Penny Stock Trading for Beginners, Dummies & Idiots

By Giovanni Rigters

© **Copyright 2021 - All rights reserved.**

The content contained within this book may not be reproduced, duplicated or transmitted without direct written permission from the author or the publisher.

Under no circumstances will any blame or legal responsibility be held against the publisher, or author, for any damages, reparation, or monetary loss due to the information contained within this book, either directly or indirectly.

Legal Notice:

This book is copyright protected. It is only for personal use. You cannot amend, distribute, sell, use, quote or paraphrase any part, or the content within this book, without the consent of the author or publisher.

Disclaimer Notice:

Please note the information contained within this document is for educational and entertainment purposes only. All effort has been executed to present accurate, up to date, reliable, complete information. No warranties of any kind are declared or implied. Readers acknowledge that the author is not engaging in the rendering of legal, financial, medical or professional advice. The content within this book has been derived from various sources. Please consult a licensed professional before attempting any techniques outlined in this book.

By reading this document, the reader agrees that under no circumstances is the author responsible for any losses, direct or indirect, that are incurred as a result of the use of information contained within this document, including, but not limited to, errors, omissions, or inaccuracies.

Table of Contents

Introduction

Chapter 1: Fundamentals of Stock Trading
What Are Stocks?
Stocks and Equity Ownership
Earnings from a Stock
Where to Buy Stocks
How to Buy Stocks
Bulls vs. Bears
Crash and Correction
Stock Indexes

Chapter 2: What Are Penny Stocks?
What Are Penny Stocks?
Characteristics of Penny Stocks
Advantages of Penny Stocks
Disadvantages

Chapter 3: How to Find the Right Broker
Who Are Brokers?
Types of Brokers
How to Select the Right Broker

Chapter 4: Buying and Selling Penny Stocks
Things to Consider Before Buying Stocks

Chapter 5: Developing a Strategy and Doing Your Research

How to Develop a Strategy

Understanding Market Behavior: Catalysts

How to Conduct Research

Chapter 6: Picking the Right Penny Stock

Chapter 7: Trading Strategies

Stock Selection

Set a Quantity Limit

Utilizing Tips and Information

Beware of Stock Promoters

Perfect Your Timing

Pay Attention to the Disclaimers

Don't Get Attached

Chapter 8: Fundamental Analysis

The Purpose of Fundamental Analysis

Quantitative vs. Qualitative

The Basis of Qualitative Fundamental Analysis

The Basis of Quantitative Fundamental Analysis

Balance Sheet

Quantitative Fundamental Analysis Systems

Chapter 9: Technical Analysis

Analysis Styles

How You Can Use Technical Analysis

Chapter 10: Risk Management

Basics of Risk Management in Penny Stock Trading

How to Avoid Being Scammed

Chapter 11 Mistakes Investors Make

Finding the Right Broker

Lack of Trading Plan

Respect Your Instincts

Ignoring Risks

Have a Strong Routine

Not Working with a Mentor

Bear in Mind Position Sizes

Chasing after Performance

Treat Trading as a Business

Learn to Accept Losses

Do not Underestimate Your Abilities

Conclusion

References

Introduction

One of the most misunderstood concepts in the world of trading is penny stocks. These stocks are a very lucrative option if you play your cards right. However, most people don't bother investing in these stocks because of the myths and misconceptions surrounding them.

This book explains everything you need to know about penny stocks in order to get started. The following chapters are carefully crafted to help you develop a proper understanding of penny stocks and learn how to safely invest in them. You can substantially increase your profits with penny stocks which wouldn't be as easy to do with other methods of trading.

The very first chapter will go into detail about the fundamentals of trading in general. You'll study what the different stock exchanges are and what the most commonly used terms mean. For an absolute beginner, the terms bear and bull might seem like complicated concepts that are hard to grasp. However, once you've read the very detailed explanations in this book, you'll know exactly what each and every term means.

It's very important to be quick and open to change when trading. We'll be looking at the various strategies you can use to make the most out of your investment. You should be careful and patient while trading penny stocks, which also applies to any type of trading. After you're familiar with all the different methods, you'll be able to devise new ones that better serve your specific purposes.

The volatility of penny stocks is usually a turn-off for most new investors, but we'll be exploring why volatility can be quite beneficial. The way that penny stocks are traded is often very different from the usual stock trading that most people are familiar with. In order to get you accustomed to the most common trading practices involved in penny stocks, this book will briefly touch on every practice that may confuse beginners.

The very first problem newbies to the penny stock market usually face finding the right broker, and this decision can have a drastic impact on your future in this market. While most other books will gloss over this issue, in this book, we will explore it in detail. The chapter on finding the right broker will go into the many nuances of selecting a broker. The various elements that go into selecting the right broker will be carefully laid out and evaluated.

Buying and selling penny stocks is another area that can get complicated due to the fact that it's very different from trading in the regular stock market. You need to understand how selling penny stocks works and which processes are involved. The chapter on this very issue will go into detail on how you can sell your penny stocks and how much effort it usually takes. Being equipped with this knowledge is greatly beneficial since it'll allow you to have a good understanding of the entire process before actually investing any of your hard-earned money.

It also takes a considerable amount of research to make the right decisions on which penny stocks you need to buy. If you're a beginner, the chances are you don't have a clue on where to start. This book will help you come up with your own research strategies so that you only invest your money in the most profitable penny stocks. We'll be exploring terms like catalysts, pumps and dumps, and much more. Another very important aspect of trading in general, chart analysis, will be explained to you in this book.

Picking the right penny stock to trade is very important, but so is trading them at the right time. If you make a wrong trade, it could result in a significant loss. If you don't understand how to trade wisely, you risk seeing your portfolio vanish into thin air. The chapter dedicated to trading and the different trading strategies will help you decide if you should hold on to a stock or if you should let it go.

You'll develop a great understanding of all the different types of analyses, including fundamental analysis and technical analysis. These will help you arrive at better decisions when it comes to buying, selling, or holding your penny stocks. With the analysis techniques detailed in this chapter, you'll be able to properly assess which stocks are worth your time and which ones you should avoid at all costs. One of the areas where this book excels is at teaching you to analyze a stock from different perspectives. This helps you gain new insights that will allow you to make better decisions.

Another aspect that's very important for any kind of trading is risk management. Unfortunately, this is one of the most ignored aspects of trading, and any investor who fails to properly identify and manage their risks is very likely to eventually suffer a massive loss. This book will walk you through the most reliable risk management strategies often used by penny stock experts.

The importance of risk management is emphasized in the later chapters since it is always useful even when you suffer considerable losses in some of your investments.

This book serves as a comprehensive guide to penny stocks that covers almost everything that a beginner needs to know to turn a profit. Both beginners and experienced traders can gain a lot from this book. Each and every piece of advice has been thoroughly researched and presented with exceptional clarity.

Penny stocks trading is very tricky to get right no matter how experienced you are. This book will help you navigate the ins and outs of the trading world and equip you with everything you need to know to make significant returns on your investments.

Chapter 1: Fundamentals of Stock Trading

Stock trading can be a fantastic way for you to save up money for retirement or add an extra source of monthly income. You have probably heard about how the stock market made people millionaires overnight but also how it made millionaires flat-broke overnight.

Without a doubt, it is an extremely unstable and volatile market. However, this extreme nature of the stock market can be used for your benefit if you are willing to take the time to understand it. If you dive into stock trading without properly understanding the basics, you might have some success, but you will more likely run into more problems than profits.

This introductory chapter will cover everything you need to know about how the stock market works, how you can begin as an investor, what you need to be aware of and how you can turn a profit. Subsequent chapters will dive into more details about each specific area.

Stock trading is a lot like law or medicine in that it is a field that is constantly changing, so you will need to stay up to date. Stock trading today is very different from what it was twenty years ago. Ideally, you should supplement your education on the subject with information from various sources and study whatever specific areas of interest in depth.

What Are Stocks?

Generally, people understand owning the stock as owning a part of the company. While this is true, it's not exactly what you might think it is.

When a company is in need of more capital, generally needed when the company is scaling up rapidly and needs more money to invest in itself, the organization has the option to 'go public.' This means that a privately owned company will now transition to becoming a public company by way of an Initial Public Offering (IPO).

By becoming a public limited company, the organization is now allowing the general public to purchase its shares and become entitled to ownership of the company and part of the profits that. The IPO process determines the price of the shares that the company will offer at the time it goes public. There are many other factors that play a part in the price of a share when a company goes public, but the bottom line is that you can become a part of the company and be a recipient of a share of its profits by purchasing its shares.

It's not necessary to purchase shares at the time of IPO, and some people would advise you to only buy shares of a company that has a proven track record on the stock exchange. However, some people do prefer to buy shares of new companies that are just entering the stock exchange at the time of the IPO. If you choose to do this, you will need in-depth information about IPO valuations.

By and large, the majority of all stock trading that goes on is for companies that already exist on the stock market. A stock is a form of security that is issued by the company, much like a currency that is issued by a state bank, and this entitles you to have the right to make decisions in the company and to also earn a profit when the company itself earns a profit. The smallest unit of a company's issued stock is a share.

So, when someone says that they own a hundred stocks, that could mean that they own a hundred shares in one specific company, or they may own varying amounts of stocks in different companies.

When they say they own a hundred shares, this could mean they own shares in a stock of a certain company or that they own shares in various other financial instruments such as mutual funds, exchange-traded funds, and limited partnerships.

Essentially, the terms stocks, shares, and equity are commonly used interchangeably, but there are differences that you should know if you want to start trading.

When you go out to buy shares in the stock of a company, you have the option to purchase either common stock or preferred stock. If you purchase common stock, you have the right to vote at company shareholder meetings and play your part in certain decisions that are made by the company. You are also eligible to receive profit in the form of dividends whenever the company issues payments for them. Some companies choose to pay dividends monthly, some quarterly, and some annually.

If you choose to purchase preferred stock, you will have a higher claim on earnings and dividends of the company at the expense of losing the right to vote in company matters. A higher claim on the earnings means that you are paid earlier than common stockholders, and in the case that the company ceases to exist and has to be liquidated, you will be paid and prioritized over common stockholders.

Stocks and Equity Ownership

When it comes to the ownership of the company as a stockholder, it can be more easily understood by understanding the nature of the company itself.

Public corporations are legally recognized as separate entities. You can think of them as something similar to humans but not quite. In effect, companies have the right to own property, they can own assets, they can borrow money, and they even file taxes. This is why if a company goes bankrupt and owes money to other companies and organizations, it is the company that is responsible and not the thousands of individual shareholders. This is known as limited liability, and it is there to ensure that the rights and interests of both the company and the shareholders are protected.

As a shareholder, you are not directly an owner of the company's assets. The company itself is the owner of its assets, such as the building it operates from. However, you are an owner of the stock that the company has issued to the stock exchange.

So, let's assume you own 20% of the shares in a company. If the company goes under, you won't have to pay 20% of what the company owes. Instead, the price of your shares will fall, which is still a loss, but it is a limited liability and is a result of the poor financial state of the company.

Moreover, the fact that the company is a separate entity on its own and that you are a shareholder of the company-issued stock also leads to the concept of separation of ownership and control. As a shareholder, you have ownership of the stocks you own, and this gives you some control over certain decisions in the company, which are influenced by shareholder votes but being a shareholder doesn't mean that you own the assets of the company itself or that you are liable for their loss.

Earnings from a Stock

Once you have bought stocks and you have invested money into the company, you now have a company-issued asset that is tradable on the stock exchange. Usually, when you buy a stock in a company, you are issued a physical certificate that identifies you as the owner of a certain number of shares in a specific company or in a portfolio of companies. However, physical certificates are becoming less common, and now things are recorded electronically. A digital database is simply updated with all your information, credentials, the number of shares you bought and their price at the time you purchased.

Primarily, there are two ways that stocks can make you money. The first is that you simply buy a stock at a low price and hold on to it, waiting for it to rise in value. When you are happy with the new, appreciated value, you can sell it for a profit. This is known as the capital gain strategy.

The second method is more challenging, but it can be far more profitable. It is trading stocks, buying low, selling high, then buying low, and then selling high. For this technique to be successful, experienced stock traders trade in stocks that are highly volatile.

These are usually stocks in companies that are either going through turbulent periods or are in industries that are volatile. Usually, slow-growing stock options like blue-chip companies offer slow and steady growth and are suitable for people who are interested in putting their money away into safe investments that will mature in 10, 20, or 30 years. This is known as the dividend strategy.

Where to Buy Stocks

Stock exchanges are where you can buy and sell stocks and shares of public companies. When a company goes public, its stock becomes available on the public stock exchange for an eligible person to buy. Once the company has sold all of its stock, private owners of shares then trade among themselves. It is important to note that companies do not buy or sell their own stocks on the stock exchange. When you are purchasing stocks from the exchange, you are buying stocks from other individual sellers who are willing to sell. Similarly, when you sell a stock, you aren't selling it back to the company but rather to other people who are interested in buying it at your sale price.

Some of the most prominent stock exchanges in the world are the New York Stock Exchange (NYSE), the National Association of Securities Dealers Automated Quotations (NASDAQ), also based in New York City, the Shanghai Stock Exchange (SSEC), the biggest in China, and the London Stock Exchange Group (FTSE-100) the largest in the UK.

Generally, when people come together, they are trading local shares on their local exchanges. This means that people who are trading on NYSE and NASDAQ are mostly trading shares of American-based companies which are registered with that specific stock exchange.

In most cases, it is not possible to trade the shares of foreign companies on a local exchange, so if you wanted to trade the shares of a Chinese company on an American exchange, it wouldn't be possible. Although, some new developments in stock exchanges are trying to pave the way for people to interact with other exchanges all over the world.

You also have the option to buy stocks from what are known as Over Counter (OTC) markets. These behave similarly to regular larger exchanges. However, they are home to smaller companies and are less regulated than the larger formal exchanges. The formal stock exchanges such as NYSE and NASDAQ have several requirements in order for companies to be eligible to sell their stocks. In contrast, OTC markets have far fewer requirements and easily accept companies that have been delisted from formal exchanges.

Another option is known as the Pink Sheets. This is also a stock trading market that doesn't require companies to be listed with the Securities and Exchange Commission (SEC). This platform is also quite lenient in its eligibility requirements and is far cheaper for companies to trade through. These markets come pose their own threats.

Some companies also choose to sell some of their stock through privately held auctions and trades, though these are usually for very specific kinds of stock and are only intended for a very small audience.

How to Buy Stocks

If you are interested in buying stocks in a company, you will need to go through a broker who can facilitate this trade for you on the stock exchange. Even though you have the option to buy directly from the exchange, it can be quite expensive and will require you to go through a lot of paperwork. The stockbrokers will have already done that to make it easy for their clients. Stockbrokers are registered with the stock exchange either directly or through a brokerage firm and are authorized traders on behalf of clients.

When it comes to finding the right broker for you, it depends on the kinds of services you need and whether or not you want to be making financial decisions on your own. Thanks to the Internet and digital trading platforms, investors now have the option to invest directly and can trade completely on their own. The two types of brokers you can use are full-service brokers or discount brokers.

As the name suggests, full-service brokers are those who give you the complete range of services which includes financial advice, insights into stock performance and future aspects of a certain stock. They basically act as your personal financial advisor on everything you are doing in and out of the stock exchange.

On the other hand, discount brokers allow you to have more control over your trades and give you the reins where you can set the selling price and decide for yourself what you want to purchase. Nearly everything is at your disposal through discount brokers, but they simply act as a gateway through which you can access the stock exchange.

With full-service brokers, you can expect to pay a much higher fee. Some full-service brokers charge an annual membership fee, take a cut on each transaction and even charge a percentage on your entire portfolio.

Discount brokers are cheaper; they have very low fees per transaction and rarely charge membership fees. Full-service brokers also often have a minimum deposit amount, whereas discount brokers allow you to trade with as little or as much money as you like.

The best strategy is to look around for all available options and shortlist brokers with a fee you can afford and a deposit that you can fulfill. Don't settle for the first broker you find. Find one that provides the kind of services you need.

These days you also have the option to invest your money through what is known as Robo-advisors. These are basically algorithms that constantly review the financial markets and then give you advice according to different preset criteria. You can discuss your goals with your Robo-advisor, and they will give you input that is likely to meet those goals given the current market performance.

Bulls vs. Bears

You may have heard people saying that the market is bullish today or that the bears are having a great day.

If the market is bearish or is favoring bear traders, this means that the stock prices are falling. They could be falling at any rate, but generally, anything over 15% is considered bearish. This indicates that people are selling stock which is causing the prices to fall. A bearish trend is not based on any one specific stock but across a range of indexes that cover various industries. On a day when the market is bearish, the overall price of stocks in the exchange will be low or falling low.

On the other hand, bullish markets represent the confidence that investors have. It means that people are confident in the economy, they are buying stock, and prices are going up.

While both of these states of the market represent the condition of the stock exchange itself, they can also be used to evaluate the overall health of the external economy. Good investments in the economy, good economic performance, and profitable forecasts induce a bullish market. On the other hand, fear, uncertainty, economic loss, and natural disasters cause a bearish market.

While these trends are frequently changing and one phase of bullish behavior will be followed by another phase of bearish behavior, bullish phases generally tend to last much longer than bearish trends.

Crash and Correction

If you've heard the phrase "a market crash," essentially what it means is that the market has dropped by more than 10%. The main difference between a crash and a bearish market is the fact that crashes typically happen within a single day or a few days.

A market is considered bearish when it is gradually losing value, a percent or two a day, and when it loses more than 15%-20% as compared to its previous high, it is considered bearish. Generally, crashes can lead to a bearish market over the course of the next few days or even weeks, but trends can also reverse themselves, and things can move to a more bullish trend.

For people who are in it for the long term, crashes are not that big of a concern because sooner or later, the market will stabilize, and things will move in an upward direction. However, certain crashes that focus on a particular industry or a company can be left frozen for quite a while. Sometimes these stocks can take months to come back up to their original highs.

Corrections are when the market stabilizes itself from a burst of growth or a crash. Sometimes stock prices plummet or skyrocket, and both of these scenarios are exceptional cases, yet quite common. When the stock price returns to its natural course of growth, this is known as a correction.

Stock Indexes

As a new stock trader, one of the most important and easy-to-understand statistics in the stock exchange are stock indices (AKA indexes). Stock indexes represent the behavior of various different stocks and give you an overview on which direction stock prices for a certain group of stock, or an industry, are headed.

When you hear people saying that the stock market is sinking like a rock in the ocean, what they are usually referring to is the fact that the index of a certain category of products is in a downward trend. Some of the major indexes include the S&P 500 and the Dow Jones Industrial Average (DJIA).

When looking at indexes, be sure to keep an eye out for the type and number of companies that they represent. DJIA, for example, is price-weighted for only thirty companies, whereas the S&P 500 is a reference for 500 of the largest companies in the US. In a stock market where there are thousands of companies, the more companies an index covers, the more accurate it will be.

Along with the representation of an index, it's also important to keep an eye out for how the index is connected to the companies it represents. Some indexes such as DJIA are price-weighted indexes meaning that the overall index is influenced by the market price of the shares of each company that it represents. Market-cap indexes reflect the total market capitalization of each of its constituents rather than the individual share price. Each index has its own advantages and drawbacks, and it all depends on how you are evaluating the market as a whole and on how you plan to use this information.

Chapter 2: What Are Penny Stocks?

Just like there are different genres in film or music that help you understand what to expect from the content you're about to consume, a similar thing occurs with stocks. The equivalent to genres in trading is stock classes.

These classes or divisions help an investor understand what to expect from stocks in terms of volatility, price, and overall market behavior. You may be thinking, "It's all stock. Why does it matter?" Well, you'd be correct about it all being stock, but each class of stock plays by different rules because of the companies that control that specific market.

Needless to say, this is only limited to the specifics of the market rather than the general rules of trading. To gain a better understanding of this chapter, it is essential that you have the past chapter fresh in your mind as you approach learning more about penny stocks.

What Are Penny Stocks?

As the name suggests, penny stocks are low-priced stocks. More specifically, they're stocks that are traded under $5 according to the U.S. Securities and Exchange Commission's (SEC) regulations. Naturally, companies that own this type of stock are small, have little earnings, sometimes none, and value-wise, they are generally undesirable. After all, a low stock price is a bad indicator, sometimes at least. In most cases, these companies can't live up to their own value due to their unstable history, their lack of experience, or their poor prospects.

Not to mention, most penny stock companies aren't listed on trading platforms, like the New York Stock Exchange (NYSE). Instead, they are traded in over-the-counter networks where the prices are highly dependent on brokers.

Over the years, penny stocks have gained a bad reputation. They are seen as a scam. The truth is the differences between penny stocks and regular stocks are just technicalities. The only scams are from companies who advertise their own stocks through newsletters to drive up their stock prices.

Granted, not being listed does impact market transparency, and we'll get to that in a moment. However, there is no truth to the belief that penny stocks are a scam. In fact, those who know the ins and outs of the penny stock market make a lot of money in little time. That said, keep in mind that, as with anything, there are advantages and disadvantages to trading penny stocks.

Characteristics of Penny Stocks

These three characteristics are what set penny stocks apart from the other stock classes. They either drive investors toward them or away from them. As an investor, you should take the time to consider what you're willing to accept and what you don't want to deal with. That way, you'll be able to make more educated decisions.

Price

As we mentioned, the defining factor of penny stocks is their price. A quick search for penny stock companies will show you that the share price can go from under one dollar to just under the five-dollar mark. Meaning, rather than spending $400+ on one regular stock, you'll be spending much less on penny stocks, which provides some sense of security and control.

Of course, there still are risk factors, but what's worse, losing $10 on one share or $0.20 on ten shares? Investing small amounts of money will simply limit your losses rather than hit you where it hurts. It's the perfect low-cost, small-scale investment if you put in the time and effort necessary to research the companies you're investing in. All in all, the low price is a penny stock's defining factor and its greatest perk, especially if you wish to invest but can't afford regular stocks.

Liquidity

Low liquidity is one of the less enticing characteristics of penny stocks. When investing in any type of stock, liquidity is always a valuable characteristic to watch out for as it translates to low risk. In case you don't already know this by heart, high liquidity means that a stock can easily be bought and sold without impacting its market price. Penny stocks aren't liquid, at least not the majority, which means you won't always have a buyer lined up to take the stocks off your hands. Unfortunately, this low liquidity is often present regardless of the stock price. Your stock price may be at an all-time high, but even that won't guarantee that you'll be able to sell.

Keep in mind that the penny stocks are the little leagues. You don't see penny stock companies on the daily news, and they have no reputation except among investor circles. In fact, most people only know of these companies because of their trading activities and not their success.

Apart from this factor which affects the demand for shares, there's also the matter of the companies themselves being small and not particularly stable. Who would want to invest in an unstable company unless they know what they're doing? This all plays into how easy it is to buy or sell shares.

The penny stock market is not a great place to own illiquid shares because of how volatile it is. That is another thing you will have to take into account. The good news is, you can always create a solid investment plan that minimizes foreseeable risks and maximizes rewards. Plus, with time, you'll learn which penny stock companies qualify as liquid and which don't.

With this acquired feel of the market, you'll be able to adapt quickly.

Volatility

The penny stock market is volatile. There are no two ways about it. Keep in mind that stability differs from predictability. Volatile means unstable rather than unpredictable. All markets are unpredictable to a certain extent, but a lot of them are relatively stable. Look at the share price history of Apple Inc. or Amazon.com, Inc.

There are little fluctuations, but look at the big-picture, and you'll see that their graphs show a slow and steady incline. Apple stock went up 48.51% in the year from 15 June 2020 to 11 June 2021. When you compare that to the stock price of a company like Entravision Communications Corp., which went up 235.76% between those exact dates, you can see exactly how sharp the market changes are.

That said, the volatility is neither negative nor positive. It's simply a double-edged sword. You could win big one day and lose big on the next. More importantly, this volatility, combined with a lack of liquidity, can have a strong impact on how much you make on a trade.

Holding an illiquid position may land you in a tight spot when you're trying to sell in order to cut your losses. Now, this volatility didn't come out of nowhere. It's the result of several factors.

First, the stocks are of a lesser value than the "big league" companies with high-priced stocks. In other words, the penny stock market is smaller because not many people want to invest in small companies. As a general rule, the weight of a market change is inversely proportional to the size of the market. Let's simplify this a little.

In a company owned by four people, each one owns 25%. Meanwhile, in a company owned by a hundred people, each one owns 1%. The penny stock market is similar to the company owned by four. Any small action has a great impact which results in a hypersensitive market.

The second factor that will be addressed in greater detail later in the chapter is manipulation. The penny stock market is easy to manipulate, but not because investors are dumb or impressionable. It's a combination of over-eagerness to take advantage of the volatility, careful advertising, and cheap shares, which present a low-cost investment. This combination further fuels the volatility, leading to abrupt price peaks and dips.

Last, but not least, news. People are sensitive to the news. When some investors learn that a civil action lawsuit is being filed against a large company, they sell or buy shares depending on the company's chances of winning the case. There are other investors, however, who believe in the core value of a company. In other words, if it's a good company, it'll bounce back. In the regular market, this could reduce/increase the value of a stock by a number of cents in a couple of days or a few dollars in a week. In the penny stock market, value-based long-term investments aren't as popular.

Combined with a hypersensitive market, a slight increase in selling or buying can cause great spikes or dips. The price change, while impactful, is often only temporary. Abnormal prices eventually return to their "normal" range.

Over-the-Counter Market

The type of market in which a stock is traded plays a big role in defining a stock's class, market behavior and characteristics. This is why it's important to understand OTC networks before analyzing the characteristics of penny stocks and comparing advantages and disadvantages.

Ordinarily, stocks are traded on the stock exchange, which is a centralized platform used by everyone who chooses to trade in a specific registered stock. There, you have one fluctuating stock price available to everyone, open access to any registered company's financial data, and a great deal of transparency.

In order to regulate these trading platforms, the SEC has set specific requirements for the companies trading there. These regulations, like a minimum amount of assets, market capitalization and extensive amounts of paperwork, are often the reasons why several major companies choose to trade OTC.

Most penny stock companies don't trade in OTC networks out of choice. A lot of them fail to meet the requirements for standardized exchanges. Meanwhile, OTC markets are not as strict, and they have much lower listing standards.

These factors make OTC markets easier for startups, small businesses, and financially struggling companies to get into. From there, these companies can issue shares that get traded by the public.

Now that you understand the characteristics of penny stocks and how their trading platforms operate, it's time to delve deeper into how this could be of potential benefit or harm to you as an investor.

Advantages of Penny Stocks

High Reward

Investments are low cost with high returns in a short window of time. Where do you sign up? There's no doubt you will reap the rewards of good investments thanks to the low prices and the volatility of the market. Although, in order to make good decisions, you need two things: a good grasp of the market feel and a good strategy. The strategy will help you decide what to buy, how much to buy when to buy, and even when to sell. Having a feel for the market will help you time your trades and fine-tune your own educated predictions.

Keep in mind, high reward in penny stocks sometimes means buying a hundred shares valued at $0.30 and waiting for a $0.10 increase. It can also mean sticking by an investment for a while, even as its value drops, and resisting the urge to sell until the company makes it big due to a sector-wide change in policy, production methods, public image, etc.

Ground Floor Investment Opportunities

There is no rule that dictates that a penny stock must remain a penny stock. A significant number of companies with low-priced shares trading OTC are startups that cannot afford to meet the requirements of stock exchanges.

By investing in those up-and-coming companies that have steadily increased earnings, customer base, and profit margins, you could potentially be one of those lucky few who get to watch a start-up grow into a big company. You'll only need research, strategy, and complete control over your emotions.

Statistics show that only 30% of business veterans manage to get their startups off the ground. As for first-time entrepreneurs, only 10% make it. These figures are worth keeping in mind when it comes to investing in startups. Don't lose sight of the fact that there is a vast difference between long-term and short-term trading strategies.

Disadvantages

High Risk

Volatility cuts both ways. Let's take a look at a case study:

In 2016 and the first half of 2017, there was a buzz around the cannabis industry in Canada prior to the 2017 Cannabis act, which legalized its use and sale. Many investors started operating on speculation, pouring a lot of their funds into up-and-coming cannabis companies, like General Cannabis Corp.

The company, initially valued at $0.75, started trading at $8.06 in January 2018. A month later, the reality of the situation sank in. Companies were forced to slow down due to regulations. Many were kept waiting months to be licensed and approved. What added to the investors' frustration, cannabis-based products, like edibles, pills, oils, etc., weren't legal at the time. They were only legalized a year later.

Alongside the restrictions in the U.S., trade regulations in Canada, and the tax rates on these companies, the lack of results led to a severe price dip. By February 2018, the company was trading at $3.78. On the 14th of June 2021, the company's stocks were valued at $0.68.

The volatility can cause you to lose all that you invested in less than a month. Professional investors know when to back out and when to go all in. They also understand that the effect of the media hype is temporary. This level of sobriety only comes with experience in the market.

Lack of Available Information

Penny stocks that trade in OTC markets can be described as a double whammy. Think of why a company may list itself in a loosely regulated market where it's not legally required to make public updated or extensive financial documents. If the company is listed in the Pink Sheets (an OTC market), it's not required to give any information to its investors. One reason that comes to mind is that the company is in financial turmoil. Take into account that some OTC companies trade their stock while going through bankruptcy proceedings.

Of course, not all companies trading in over-the-counter markets are inches away from bankruptcy. However, the lack of available financial information is a major disadvantage when it comes to trading penny stocks. Without enough information, any decision you make won't fall under trading as much as it will fall under outright gambling.

The easiest way to dodge this disadvantage is to invest in the penny stocks listed in NASDAQ, NYSE, and the other regulated stock exchanges. Another way is to invest in companies that provide extensive information. In other words, don't make any blind trades without fully accepting the nature of the risk you're taking.

Probability of Fraud

We mentioned earlier that the penny stock market could be easily manipulated because it's highly responsive to media hype. How can you fall victim to this risk? The answer is, in many ways. So many schemes have been employed to the extent that they have names now. The most common three are:

The Pump-and-Dump: Some people buy a certain stock in an unknown company, then pay finance blogs to nudge inexperienced investors towards that company. Once the share price reaches a high enough level, they sell and make their money, i.e., dump. Because the hype was the only factor keeping the stock price high, the price falls quickly once the hype dies down, harming everybody but the people that set it up in the process.

The Expert: Some scammers take advantage of the misconception that penny stocks are how you can retire at 30. All they do is create a website, some story about how they have retired at the age of 32 to lure you in with content and keep you hooked. Now, early retirement is a possibility for you because you've paid for their newest online course.

Plus, their weekly newsletters, loaded with market insights, are now all over your inbox. What are they really doing? One, they could be pumping for the pump-and-dumpers. Two, they know nothing about stocks. They're just good at giving the impression that they're experts

The Short-and-Distort: Last but not least, this scam is a mix between short-selling and defamation. Here, the scammer borrows stocks, then sells them at the original price. If the price drops, they buy back the stocks at the lower price, return them to the lending party, and keep the difference (original price - lower price).

Just as there are many risks, there are also many ways to avoid them. You will learn each and every one of them by the end of this book.

As you proceed to the next chapter, here is something you should keep in mind. Penny stocks are a challenging stock class. They require time and attention. In the short term, if you have the right strategies, you'll win big.

If you're looking to make long-term investments, you'll either lose massively or become one of the first investors in a strong rising company. Some might be thinking, "Yeah, right. A penny stock company will become the next Microsoft." What you should be thinking is, "Why not?" All companies have to start somewhere. When it first joined the stock market in 1981, Apple opened the year with $0.15/share. Monster Energy, the beverage company, started in December 1985 with $0.13/share. As of 11 June 2021, the company is worth well over $49 billion.

The point is, you can make it big in the trading world, whether you're trading regular stocks or the more intimidating penny stocks. You only need to be willing to learn, take risks, and make mistakes because the truth is, there is always a risk. Every single trader thinks they can get in and out scot-free, and they usually get disappointed early on. Some end up quitting. Others end up losing their money by letting their fear, greed, and disappointment guide their investment choices. Economist Benjamin Graham boiled this down to, "Successful investing is about managing risk, not avoiding it."

Chapter 3: How to Find the Right Broker

Investing in stocks can be extremely rewarding but, at the same time, it can also be very risky. Warren Buffett said, "If you don't find a way to make money while you sleep, you will work until you die." The stock market offers you the opportunity to amplify your wealth, but it isn't as easy as it seems. To make the right investment decisions, there are a lot of factors that have to be considered and to make smart investment choices, one has to invest a lot of time and effort into understanding the nuances of the stock market.

Managing your investment portfolio and constantly following the stock market can take up a lot of your time, which, unless you are a professional trader, can become quite inconvenient and taxing. This is where brokers come in. A broker can help you maintain your investment portfolio and also provide you with valuable insights and advice on how you can profit the most through your investments.

Considering that a broker will more or less be responsible for managing and making investments for you, selecting the right broker is essential. This chapter will walk you through the process of selecting the right broker.

Who Are Brokers?

Stock Brokers are essentially middlemen who enable you to make investments by purchasing and selling stocks on your behalf. Financial transactions have to be performed through a broker. However, brokers not only sell and purchase shares on your behalf, but they are also in a position to provide expert advice on where you should invest your money to get the best possible return.

This is because they follow the market very closely and understand its ins and outs. Their expert advice does come at a cost. They charge commissions for their services which can vary from one broker to the next. The stock market is well regulated, and brokers have to be registered.

They usually function as part of a brokerage firm, and there are three main types of brokerage firms. Selecting the right type of broker is important, and your decision should be based on the nature of trading you want to engage in.

Types of Brokers

There are different kinds of brokerage services, and they all have their upsides and downsides. The right one for you solely depends on the type of trading you are interested in. What sets these brokers apart is mainly the kind of services that they offer and the commission they charge. The amount of flexibility that is offered to the client while making trades also varies from one type of broker to the next.

Full-Service Brokers

As the name suggests, Full-Service Brokers offer the complete service. They charge the highest commission. When you sign up with a full-service brokerage company, it will usually assign you a dedicated stockbroker. These companies tend to have their own in-house research and analysis wings that provide their clients with valuable insights into the investment market.

They also provide banking services and numerous other benefits that make purchasing and selling stocks effortless. With a Full-Service Brokerage company, you don't have to get in touch with your assigned stockbroker every time you need to make a trade. You are generally offered the option to make your trade through your account via a computer or a dedicated mobile application.

Discount Broker

Discount brokers offer various services similar to full-service brokers but charge smaller commissions. They offer access to stocks, mutual funds, and banking facilities. Discount brokers will probably be more attractive to active traders as they tend to provide higher flexibility than Full-Service Brokers.

Online Brokers

Online brokers, in addition to charging the lowest commission, also offer direct access, which is why they are also referred to as direct access stockbrokers. The commission they charge is usually priced according to the stock that you invest in but can also be charged per trade.

In addition to the commission that they charge, there is usually a monthly subscription fee that is associated with the online account. However, the subscription fee also depends on the number of monthly transactions you perform. The monthly subscription fee has an inverse relationship with the number of trades that are performed, which can be advantageous to active traders.

The direct access platforms that are provided by online brokers give you access to graphing and research tools, which makes them the most attractive option for active traders who like to closely follow the investment market. They even provide access to electronic communication networks, which let you perform trading without the involvement of a third party. They also offer the advantage of faster trading, which lets you make near-instant investments at the click of a button.

How to Select the Right Broker

Selecting the right broker for your trading needs becomes simpler once you know the services offered by different types of brokers. However, there are other parameters that you should also consider before making your decision. Here are a few tips that can help you select the right broker for you.

Reputation

Before you decide to go with a particular broker, the first thing that you must check is the reputation of the broker. Fortunately, this is one aspect that is easy to evaluate. The simplest way of gauging the background and reputation of a broker is to read up on the experiences of their existing and past customers. This can be done by referring to the reviews and complaints provided by their clients.

The number of clients that a broker has is also a good indication of their reputation. If you decide to make your investments through an online platform, you should check the ratings of the companion mobile app by users on Google Play or the Apple App Store.

Commission

Different brokers charge different commissions. Naturally, the broker that charges the least commission charges will be the most attractive option for you. However, when evaluating different brokers based on their commission charges, you shouldn't make your decision simply based on the amount, but you must weigh the commission charges against the services offered.

In addition to the regular commission that brokers charge, there can be a lot of hidden charges as well, which you must watch out for. These hidden charges are something that may not be mentioned at first, and you must specifically ask the representative to declare any hidden costs.

Services Offered

The kind of services offered varies, not just depending on the kind of broker that you opt for, but also among the same kind of brokers as well. Depending on the kind of trading you plan on getting into, you should pay attention to the kind of research and analysis tools that the brokers offer.

Many brokers, in addition to research tools and reports, also provide learning material and small courses, which can be very useful if you are a novice investor. Even if you are an experienced investor, these courses and educational materials can help you keep up with the latest changes and developments in the market.

Customer Service

Although these days, most broker platforms are highly automated and intuitive, you never know when things can go wrong. If you are new to the stock market, you will often require expert advice and assistance during trading, and a lot of brokers provide that alongside suggestions. Opting for such a broker can simplify and enhance your trading experience. That said, the quality of customer service provided by a broker is an important thing to consider while selecting a broker.

Physical Office Locations

The Internet has taken over the world, and online brokerage facilities are very convenient to use. Even with that in mind, when selecting a broker, you must try to opt for one that has a physical office in your vicinity or, at the very least, one in your city. Usually, full-service brokers have numerous physical offices that you can go to, but when it comes to discount brokers and online brokers, these can be quite scarce.

A physical location where you can talk face to face with an expert can make your trading very convenient, especially if you are not very comfortable trading online or are new to trading. While interacting with a professional expert, you can often gain valuable insights that can help you build and enhance your portfolio.

Selecting the right broker is a crucial aspect of being successful as a trader. The process of choosing one can become quite confusing. What you need to understand is that you don't have to opt for the broker that offers you the best features or the one that charges the lowest commission.

You have to find a balance. A lot of the features and services offered may be redundant based on your experience and the kind of trading you wish to engage in. On the other hand, you may have to pay a certain premium to get access to the features that you need the most. You should select a broker according to your trading needs. That is why you need to understand the different types of brokers and the value that they bring to the table. If you keep in mind the points mentioned in this chapter and do your research well, you should be able to find a broker that meets all your requirements.

Chapter 4: Buying and Selling Penny Stocks

Penny stocks are a niche option that can suit the needs of some people but can be totally unsuitable to others. If you're someone who likes to take risks and invest in short-term stocks, penny stocks are the right choice for you. However, if you're very risk-averse and don't want to take any unnecessary gambles, then you're better off investing elsewhere.

Even though penny stocks are meant for those who don't mind taking risks, they're rather technical to deal with. You can't just buy a penny stock and forget about it like you would with any other stock. They can turn your small investment into huge profits, but only if you play your cards right. If you're not careful and analytical while investing in these, you're more likely to lose all your investment, no matter how small it is.

For the risk-takers, the potential benefits of investing in penny stocks outweigh the risks. However, it doesn't mean that the risks are insignificant or should be ignored. If you still feel like you can successfully trade in penny stocks, then maybe these tiny investments are just what you need.

If you feel like the risks are too high, then penny stocks are definitely not for you. You won't be able to successfully buy or sell penny stocks if you're not willing to take some risks. If all this advice still has not changed your mind, then you should seriously consider dealing in penny stocks. Before you get your hands dirty, you should be well aware of the basics and the tips from experts who've been trading penny stocks for a while.

Many investors are still making a good amount of money by trading in penny stocks and what separates them from those who suffer losses is that they make the right decisions. They don't view penny stocks as lotteries, and they try to implement their own knowledge and expertise while making their decisions. If you can learn from these people about which penny stocks to purchase and which ones to avoid, you'll have a much easier time breaking into the market.

Things to Consider Before Buying Stocks

You can choose to buy penny stocks from two major options. The first option that you have is the OTC (Over The Counter) market, and the other one is through stock exchanges. Most of the people who lose their money in penny stocks will choose to buy them from the OTC option. The more intelligent investor will most likely buy these stocks from more renowned companies that list their penny stocks on the various regulated stock markets.

However, the penny stocks often lie at the bottom of these regulated exchanges due to the presence of bigger companies with more significant stocks. If you choose to go with these exchanges, you're much less likely to lose your investment as compared to an unregulated OTC market. This is due to the proven track records and better strategies of the companies listed.

Penny stocks are often valued at less than $5, and this is usually due to the poor performance of the companies offering them. If you look at the OTC market, then you'll discover that the companies offering their penny stocks are usually new or suffering constant losses.

Since the penny stocks on regulated exchanges are from companies that have taken a sharp hit due to unforeseen circumstances, these companies are more likely to bounce back, and when they do, you'll be earning significantly more with them than with the larger companies.

Being present on any major exchange is an accomplishment, and it means that the company has held up to certain standards in the past. An intelligent investor looks into the history and the background of a company before they decide to invest their money. If you're buying penny stocks sold at OTC markets, then it proves that you don't pay proper attention to the results of research on a company, and you're more likely to suffer losses in the future.

Understanding Risk Money

In the penny stock circles, the term risk money is loosely thrown around, and if you don't understand what it means, then you won't know how to proceed any further. Risk money is the money that you can afford to lose without having to worry about the consequences. The newbies to penny stock trading, or any other trading for that matter, are advised to only invest risk money so that they can get a better feel of how the market works.

It's also advisable for beginners to only invest in penny stocks that are lower priced than others. This is due to the fact that you'll lack a lot of knowledge when it comes to buying and selling during the initial phases, and you're more likely to suffer losses. Once you've gained a significant amount of experience in the various tactics involved in penny stock trading, you can move to bigger and riskier ventures. Once you're an experienced player, you'll be able to take more calculated risks, which will inevitably result in higher yields.

The Easy Way to Make Good Decisions

Most people start out with penny stocks by purchasing whatever stocks seem to be profitable. These predictions often prove wrong, and they end up suffering losses. This isn't to say that you should never trust your instinct or try to buy a seemingly good penny stock. What this means is just that you need to be fully aware of what you're doing before you make a decision.

Most of the time, a newbie trader like you won't know which penny stocks to buy simply due to inexperience. You'll also not be as good as someone who's been buying penny stocks for a long time. The traders who've purchased and sold a lot of stocks will have suffered more losses than you, and they would've made more profits than you as well.

The ability of an experienced trader to look at the charts and be able to predict the future prospects of a company is uncanny.

The best course of action for you as a beginner is to follow someone who's more experienced in penny stock trading. There are plenty of apps and videos all over the Internet where penny stock veterans share their own strategies. You should try to follow these traders to learn their strategies and the stock they're investing in. If you learn by practicing someone else's strategy, then you can learn the nuances that only more advanced traders know about.

This isn't a long-term strategy, but in the beginning, you can easily borrow the ideas from someone who has a proven track record in making profits. Don't fall for any empty claims. Try to find genuine people who won't try to rip you off by selling their courses on penny stocks that promise 1000% returns.

The Mindset to Avoid

Unfortunately, most of the people who get into penny stocks do so because they're motivated by the one-off stories of someone becoming an overnight millionaire. However, stories like these rarely exist outside of fiction, and you should properly assess the reasons why you want to start penny stock trading.

If you want to make a quick buck and become a celebrity trader, then the actual results are bound to underwhelm you. However, if you can commit yourself to learning the process and suffering some setbacks while doing so, you can safely enter the penny stocks market.

You have to understand that you can't really turn a few hundred bucks into thousands of dollars and achieve financial freedom in a single go. You'll have to adjust to the reality, and the reality is that it takes time, patience, and commitment to make even the tiniest of profits.

Many people assume that penny stocks are akin to a lottery where you just have to chip in the money and wait for the magic to happen. If you're one of those people, then you can rest assured that you can chip in your money and wait, wait for it to vanish.

You have to make an educated and informed decision to actually be able to earn some profit from penny stocks. If you don't do your research and you invest your money mindlessly, then you'll lose it just as fast as you spent it. The most successful investors conduct thorough research and analyze the previous year's trends of the company whose stocks they're purchasing. Learn from them and how they chose to invest in an asset, and you'll be able to replicate the same success after some practice.

Practice Makes Perfect

One of the best ways for any newbie to enter the trading game without risking their actual investments is through "paper trading." You just have to keep track of a few stocks using a pen and paper and pretend that you actually invested in them. You won't need any money to practice this way. You just need to get a piece of paper and a pen to get started.

The imaginary portfolio will help you track the fictional profits or losses that you incur. This way, you can grow your skills really fast, and it won't cause you any financial losses either. The other hidden benefit is that you will be learning the terminologies and tips in penny stocks which will help you in the future.

Mistakes are what make the better investors better. This is a free and harmless way to make those mistakes and gain experience. Once you've paper traded for a decent amount of time, you can easily enter the exchange market with confidence. You'll not only learn how to buy penny stocks, but you'll also be able to learn when to sell them, which is a very important aspect of trading in penny stocks.

Choose Wisely

Whenever you start trading, be it in penny stocks or other larger stocks, you must remember that your choices make a world of difference. Many new investors like to go for the latest trends and invest all their money in one company that's selling its shares like hotcakes. This is not the best route ahead due to possible and sometimes inevitable complications.

You have to understand that the majority of investors in the stock market are there just to lose their money. Only a handful of investors actually make any substantial profit, and they do so because they don't rely on the advice of anyone.

While the majority of the crowd follows a popular sentiment that they heard from their friends, colleagues, acquaintances, boss, or in a bar, you have to focus on conducting in-depth research before investing your money. You don't want to follow the crowd. Most of them are heading for losses.

You can't rely on the general sentiment that prevails among people due to the unpredictability factor. If you've heard that a stock is selling really well, then almost anyone with the same interests has heard about it as well. This means that the stock will already be saturated by the time you buy it. This leads to maturation which in turn leads to overpricing of the stock.

What this means is that what goes up will come down. By the time you've heard of a stock that's booming, it'll reach its peak maturity, and the prices will take a dip. The basic rule of investing in stocks is to never take out less than you invested, but if you invest in the supposedly hot stock, then you'll witness its sudden fall, and you'll have to cash out immediately at a lower price.

Do What You Love

The old advice about following your passion surprisingly fits very well into the world of penny stock trading. If you have any doubts about the stocks you should be investing in, then go with the industry you're most passionate about. The stocks that you could be passionate about may be from any industry like music production, tourism, technology, AI, fashion, and much more.

One of the most common behaviors exhibited by investors is to ignore their own industry and interests so that they don't get biased. It's an intelligent approach to avoid your passion because you may start thinking with your heart, and in the stock market, there's no place for anything other than logic.

However, it could prove very beneficial to you if you invest in something you're passionate about because you already have adequate knowledge. This knowledge will prove extremely useful for you when you want to assess the possibilities of a company's stocks growing or dropping. This is an inherent advantage you'll have over the others who're just investing to make some profit, and you should definitely exploit it to the maximum.

Stay Attentive

Trading in stocks is unlike any regular 9 to 5 job that you may have had before. Penny stocks are one step ahead by being unlike regular trading as well since you have to be aware of the positions of your stocks at all times. This is because penny stocks are quite volatile, and they heavily depend on the smallest of market forces. You can't just leave penny stocks to mature like the stocks from well-established companies.

Penny stocks can give you huge returns, but only if you're aware of their prices at all times. You have to capitalize on any short window of opportunity where the price of your stocks is at the predicted maximum. The prices can fall drastically in a short time due to the volatile nature of penny stocks, and you just can't miss out on an opportunity because you were too lazy to be vigilant.

There are many tips and suggestions that you can implement in your newly started journey of penny stocks to get better much faster. These were some of the most important tips about buying and selling your penny stocks so that you can earn the maximum profits.

Remember, you're getting into penny stock trading only to make profits, and you should do everything to fulfill that goal. This chapter has provided you with valuable insights, and you can find even more resources to get better all over the Internet. So just keep working on your skills and timing, and the profits will soon start pouring in.

Chapter 5: Developing a Strategy and Doing Your Research

Developing a successful strategy is one of the most underrated aspects of stock trading. What the majority of new investors do is that they learn about the existing strategies, then pick the one that comes with the highest recommendations or the one that's most successful (or well-advertised).

Now, there's nothing wrong with learning from other people. After all, the reason we are where we are at this moment is that we've built on information passed onto us by those who came before us. The main problem is that new investors stop there. They pick a strategy, and they stick with it for life, or until they pick another one.

First of all, there are no presets that can help you win. Strategies are like sunglasses. You can try all of them out, but not all of them will suit you. Even if the strategies end up working for you, they're still not yours, not in terms of suitability at least. Any strategy you'll find online or in books was developed by someone else who decided that was the best way for them.

It doesn't have to be the best way for you. It could work, but what if you could do much better with a strategy created by you for you? This is what you'll learn in this chapter.

While the most common trading strategies will be covered in a different chapter, this chapter will help you learn what you need to develop your own strategy. It will also shed light on how to research various stocks, read charts, and gain a better understanding of the market. To get the most out of this chapter, you'll want to keep in mind the fundamentals of stock trading and the characteristics of penny stocks and the OTC markets. Both are key to attaining a full, detailed picture and a complete understanding.

How to Develop a Strategy

Needs

The first factor that should influence one's strategy is their needs. Keep in mind that needs are different from wants. A need is something essential to your survival. Getting your needs fulfilled isn't an option but a necessity.

Let's say you need to make a lot of money and fast. In this case, it would be better for you to invest in volatile stocks. That way, you'll make the money you need in a short window of time. However, if you need to generate steady income, volatile stocks won't help you.

You'll need to make fundamentally sound investments to carry you in the long-term while conducting thorough risk assessments to determine whether or not you can afford to invest in short-term companies. It's worth mentioning that depending on penny stocks as means of generating a steady income is a big risk if you don't know what you're doing.

Needs don't have to be strictly financial. They can also be emotional and mental. Some need or want to make money, but they value their peace of mind more. To them, relaxation is a need that they will have to sacrifice if they follow a trading strategy that requires them to be glued to their devices all day.

Others need mental stimulation, and in this case, the more engaging and challenging a strategy is, the happier they'll be. Before you move onto the next point, ask yourself, "What needs am I fulfilling by investing in penny stocks? What needs am I sacrificing?"

Wants

The things you want are luxuries. They're only there to make you live more comfortably. If you lose them, you'll still be comfortable, just not as much. It's like an extra topping on your sundae. They, too, are important to consider, but not as much as your needs. Among common wants is early retirement. It's a goal for many, and it can be achieved through various means. If you have the time, then you can fulfill your want by picking a trading strategy that guarantees you retirement by a specific age.

Another want is to make a little cash on the side. This one is common among fresh graduates who want to start building a financially sound future. For those people, they'll either want to stay away from risks and instead trade based on value or follow chart patterns. While volatile stocks may be tempting, it's important to note that you can't afford the luxury of taking risks just yet. Speaking of which, taking risks is a luxury. If what you're looking for is the adrenaline rush that comes with the fast-paced world of stocks, and you have the money for that, you can adopt a trading style that allows you to take calculated risks.

Resources

Ideally, we'll have enough time, money, and energy to fulfill our needs and wants. However, that's never really the case, is it? Compromises have to be made, and decisions must be taken. When you're considering a trading strategy, consider the resources you have. As mentioned in the example above, someone still financially starting out won't be able to afford risk-based strategies.

Meanwhile, someone who is financially secure, with a little walking-around money, can afford to take a few risks. Better the stock market than Vegas, don't you think?

Time is another essential resource that many don't have. It's the reason brokerage firms exist. If you've got the time to observe the market and learn from it, you're more likely to depend on your own understanding of market behavior alongside financial data rather than solely depending on data and analysis methods or information.

If you don't have the time, you'll need to invest in a company which you can forget about, then come back every few days until you sell your stocks for profit. It will take you many hours of research and monitoring, but in the end, you'll have a solid investment.

Personality Type

Are you driven by logic or emotion? Are you always interested in updating your knowledge and improving on your methods, or are you the type of person who would rather figure out a solid formula and then follow it until the end? It's characteristics like that which determine how suitable a certain strategy is for you. If you've figured out your wants and needs, then find a couple of strategies to fulfill them without exhausting your resources.

Your personality type will determine which one you pick. Some people can't resist looking at their stocks every day, but they also get the jitters when they see the graph dipping, and that's when they sell. If you're not yet capable of controlling your emotions, you'll want to stop checking on your stocks' performance, or you'll want to abide by a different strategy that saves you the trouble. As a logical thinker, you might think you're off the hook, but you're not.

Logical thinkers often fall prey to their belief that if they're careful, they won't lose, ever. It's an illogical belief, yet a very logical one at the same time if one believes they can account for all the variables. Either way, there are two approaches to setting a strategy based on personality. You can either let your personality type dictate your strategy or use the trading strategy you believe is best suited to your personality.

Preferences

Everyone has their preferences when it comes to learning. What interests one person may not interest another, and that's perfectly normal. One of the makings of a strong strategy is an investor's passion for honing it. You already know that the penny stock market is affected by many factors, and these are economic, political, and social.

Chances are, you already have some experience in one of these three fields. This experience makes up one of your strong suits. Your interest in a particular field makes up a second strong suit. As long as you're interested, you'll want to know more about how it works. Of course, you need to understand the basics of how the three fields affect the market, but you're also allowed to specialize. By specializing, you'll be playing to your strengths.

If you've been involved in social media long enough to understand how people react when a certain story gains "trending" status, why not use this ability to make some money? Likewise, if your experience in a specific industry has taught you how to detect potential company booms, why not put this knowledge to use? To sum up, a strong strategy plays to an investor's strength, be it skills, knowledge, personality, or resources.

Understanding Market Behavior: Catalysts

You can't begin to plan a strategy without understanding the market around you. You simply need to study the arena and what affects it before you decide on your weapon of choice.

Trading Imbalances

The market is volatile, and this has already been covered. It's all due to the low number of buyers and sellers. We'll be looking at the imbalances here as catalysts. Here's a small example of what's meant by that. At some point in time, people started buying shares from company X, and so the price went up drastically. The increase was suspiciously fast, though. What do you do?

Sell as soon as you can. Why? If the stock price goes up unnaturally, trust that it will eventually return to its original value, if not lower. You can also do the opposite if the share price has been down a little more than normal.

You can buy at a low price and sell when the market is back to its regular rates. The rule is that any unnatural spike or dip in share price caused by a trade imbalance will eventually even out, and the price will return to its original levels. It will take you quite some time to get the timing right, but once you do, you'll be able to capitalize on those sudden changes and their aftermath.

Company Growth

Growth is always a catalyst for change and a good one. No company is created with the goal of failing in mind. The better a company performs, the more it is seen as reliable. Lucrative investments increase demand which drives up prices. Whether you already have an up-and-coming company in your portfolio or are considering investing in a startup, growth is one thing you should always keep in mind.

Growth in one of the company's aspects is always good. However, overall growth across the board is even better. It's a more accurate indicator of a company's performance, and it is guaranteed to exhibit itself in the share price. In other words, if you see a company increasing its revenue, growing its customer base, and taking over its market little by little, consider investing while the stocks are affordable before the opportunity passes you by.

Industry Changes

Industries change violently and at the drop of a hat, especially new industries. Just like the cannabis industry in 2016 and 2017, a change in legislation can cause a boom as people start making their own conclusions about a company's full potential. Another change could make it harder for certain companies to exist, thus squeezing them, thinning their profit margins, and hindering their productivity. It is also what happened in Canada's cannabis industry.

The best thing about changes in the industry is that they're not dependent on one company. If a positive change affects an entire industry, all companies win without doing anything extra. When a new film camera comes out, camera lens companies start catering to the new product.

Meanwhile, movie studios win big as they start benefiting from the technology, and when studios win big, cinemas win big. In this example, the film industry is able to increase its revenue just by staying up-to-date. Did you notice how far back the effects of change can go? All the way from camera manufacturers to cinemas. To keep up with industry changes, you'll have to keep an eye on the big picture, as well as the small picture.

When the audio social platform Clubhouse launched in 2020, it pushed the social media giants, Facebook and Twitter, to use the same technology. Big picture, one needs to think about what this means for the industry. Small picture, every company reacts differently to change. Some adapt, some don't. Some adapt to the change, and they take the opportunity to become an industry leader, while others adapt by doing the bare minimum to keep up, thus becoming a follower.

Media

It cannot be overstated enough. People are highly influenced by the news. It's the main reason why markets are so volatile and easy to manipulate. We've previously discussed pump-and-dump schemes and how they're used for advertising stock to drive its prices up, allowing scammers to sell at insanely high prices.

Short-and-distort schemes employ the same tactic, but by spreading negative publicity, causing people to sell until the price is low enough for scammers to buy back their shorted stocks. That said, following the news is essential to an investor's success, as long as they're critically thinking about what they're listening to. If the news reports a merger or a contract, you'll want to think about what this means when it comes to your portfolio.

While, in most cases, it is a good thing, it's not always a good thing if you can foresee an insurmountable obstacle on the company's horizon. In this case, you'll need to alter your investment strategy in accordance with the external factors you can see.

How to Conduct Research

Learning market behavior is important, but it must be backed up by research for it to be utilized effectively to your benefit. The topic of research is a heavy one, packed with information; that's why you'll find it distributed over several chapters. These are the basic things you need in your research:

Know the Industry

Many beginner traders ignore this advice, but hopefully, this won't be you when you start trading. Trade in what you know. If there's an industry that you're familiar with, invest in its companies. Knowing the customer base, demand, supply, biggest players, biggest competitors, and the overall position of the industry will guide you through your decision-making process. Your understanding will help you understand the market, gauge performance, and make sound choices.

Meanwhile, a new industry will require you to speculate most of the time based on people's opinions, news, etc., out of a lack of knowledge. In the long-term, it's good to diversify your portfolio by investing in different industries so as to not be dependent on the performance of just one. However, before you approach new industries, you need to hone your research process by studying the industries you know.

Know the Company

Don't invest in a company because you've got a good feeling about it. Invest because you know the company. Especially when trading in penny stocks and OTC markets, you need to have as much information as you can before you make a trade. When a company catches your eye, read about it. Understand its role in the industry and how it is connected to other companies in terms of the supply chain. Understand what factors play the biggest part in shifting its stock price and know whether or not there is a lot of demand on the company's shares. If there isn't, pass up on the investment. There's no reason to buy if you can't guarantee you'll be able to sell. With this complete understanding, you'll be able to react, not to the hype, but to the company's performance.

In fact, this could help you take risks and buy when everyone else is selling. Many believe you shouldn't follow your gut when it comes to stocks, but they're wrong. You should follow your gut, just not when it has zero tangible evidence behind it. Know the company, and then your gut will lead you in the right direction.

Learn Chart Patterns

Learning how to recognize chart patterns is essential when it comes to research. Charts serve as valuable indicators to help you evaluate a company and its stock. Stock moves in one of three trends. An upward trend means that the stock price is increasing. It will still be fluctuating between highs and lows, but both values will be higher overall.

A downward trend means the exact opposite, with the stock price constantly decreasing. Consolidation is where the stock price moves up and down between a specific range of values.

Based on these trends, there are three types of patterns:

Breakout: As the name suggests, this pattern involves the price changing beyond the range it has been trading in. The breakout could be an increase in price, but it could also be a decrease.

Reversal: The market is greatly fluid, but it is quite predictable. Often the market changes direction in cycles. Uptrends are followed by downtrends. Downtrends are followed by uptrends. A reversal pattern is the repetitive uptrend-downtrend cycle.

Continuation: Sometimes, the market isn't that fluid at all. The prices could go up and down for a stretch, seemingly at random, before the range gets tighter. The price then stabilizes at a certain point for a period of time until a catalyst interferes.

Paper Trading

The last step to developing your strategy and honing your research skills is a practical one. When someone starts working at a new company, are they immediately given a big task that can impact the company's image, or are they put on probation and given tasks under supervision?

The new employee needs to get used to the company's style before they're officially a part of it so that when they are, they fit in seamlessly. Before you start trading with your money, it's important to have already developed your strategy. What you need is either an online simulator or a pen and paper. Stock charts and all sorts of information are available everywhere online. Start making your own trades and predictions, then follow the market closely to see where you were right and where you were wrong, and most importantly, why. Granted, you won't be making any money just yet, but you'll develop a concrete strategy that makes you a lot of money later on.

Chapter 6: Picking the Right Penny Stock

Penny stocks are a seemingly lucrative option that attracts most people by promising a few key advantages over regular stocks. With a penny stock, you can get started with just a little bit of money, and you can take higher risks owing to the less costly nature of these stocks. You know you don't have to risk a lot of money, and that'll provide you with a boost in confidence.

However, the difficulty with penny stocks is that it's very easy to lose your money by gambling it away. A lot of investors underestimate the value of the money they use to trade due to the low prices, and this can lead to overspending or wasteful spending.

Even though there are high risks associated with these stocks, some of the stocks that have a strong foundation go on to increase in value over the course of time. Some of these stocks will also turn into multi-baggers that can reap huge profits. However, this is especially difficult to accomplish due to the nature of penny stock trading.

It's not easy to identify a penny stock that guarantees the highest chances of success. Find the correct stock, and you can invest a lot of money without worrying about the risks. In this chapter, we're going to be looking at the various different approaches you can take to make sure you're picking the winning stock.

There are a few factors that you should know before that.

Liquidity

The most important thing you need to know before you invest in any penny stock is that they usually have low liquidity. Penny stocks don't have a very big market with huge demand. You have to consider the fact that penny stocks lack liquidity and that you'll not be able to sell them off instantly. This is because penny stocks are traded in low volumes, and these stocks have a relatively larger bid-ask spread.

Don't Be In a Hurry

Before you decide to invest all your money in penny stocks, you need to ask yourself if you're fine with the extremely high levels of risk that come with this. Everyone has a different style of investment, and you have to determine if penny stocks suit your investment style or not. If you can confidently spare a little money that'll be most likely lost, then you're ready to proceed with buying the penny stocks.

Get a Grip

Trading in penny stocks or any other stock requires you to have a clear understanding of the fundamentals of the market. The stock prices are driven by a lot of factors like natural disasters, national emergencies, government policies, global wars, elections, and much more. If you can understand how these impact penny stocks, then you can easily invest in a good one. This point becomes even more important when talking about smaller companies since they're impacted much more strongly by the various external stimuli.

This is why an investor who has been trading in any kind of stock for a while will have a much better idea of how to make the right choices. It's important to understand how penny stocks are affected because their value can be manipulated as well. You can buy stocks in bulk, and the price can increase drastically because of that.

This is because the companies offering penny stocks are rather small, and any small investment can significantly affect their stock prices. Once you've bought and increased the prices of a stock, you can sell it to make a rather large profit while the market is left confused. This is why it's important to get a grip on the fundamentals of the market so that you can make such predictions and avoid any losses.

Keep Researching

When it comes to purchasing a stock, the job of an investor who invests in mid-cap or high-cap stocks is significantly easier than the one who wishes to invest in low-cap stocks. This is because there is a handful of mid-cap and large-cap options only. However, there are hundreds of low-cap stocks which can leave anyone confused.

This is the primary reason why the strategies while buying different-sized stocks are so different. The investors buying the relatively larger stocks will usually shortlist a few companies and then analyze their fundamentals. However, you'll have to change it up a little bit so that you make the right choices for your penny stocks.

You'll need to start off with broader criteria that segregate the companies by their industry, services, sector, or any other similar criteria. Once you've created a list of stocks based on these criteria, you can start eliminating the unwanted options.

You should try to find the few companies that have the highest probability of turning into multi-baggers. As you keep practicing and trading more and more, you'll start to learn what criteria you should keep for finding out the best companies with the most potentially profitable stocks.

Paper Trade if You're Unsure

If you're still not sure about the stocks that you should be buying, it's best to start with paper trading. This concept has been discussed in detail in the previous chapters, but it's such an important tool in trading that it just can't be ignored. You should follow the stock that you're confused about and note down all its price changes, volume, and other factors on a paper or a spreadsheet. This way, you can understand if the stock you were going to pick is a profitable option or not. However, remember not to stick with paper trading for too long. Eventually, you'll have to take actual risks and buy real stocks if you want to make any significant profits at all. So, utilize the paper trade initially, as it can be an amazing tool to help you learn the ropes but just don't become overly dependent on it.

Don't Be Delusional

One of the things that most stock market newbies are unfamiliar with is the stock price and how a particular stock is valued. There's no such thing as "affordable" in any stock market as opposed to what many people might have you believe. Getting more stocks of a company for the same price as fewer stocks of another company may seem like a good idea to the uninitiated, but it's not.

You have to understand that the way that a normal investor thinks about stocks and their value is completely wrong. If you purchase more units for the same price, then don't rationalize by thinking that the potential for growth is higher, and that could mean more profits. You're supposed to think like an investor and not a gambler.

You should disregard the number of units you can buy for a particular price. You should be more focused on other factors like the company's recent performance and the potential for growth in the near future. The market price of a company's stock is something that can change drastically due to a variety of external factors, which is why you should be more focused on the core fundamentals of a company. Those are more useful as indicators in the long run.

Understand Dilution

More often than not, reputable companies issue their shares so that they can use the influx of investments to expand and grow the company. However, in the case of smaller companies, the capital may be used for other purposes like attracting better talent. This difference in intent can lead to smaller companies getting diluted in terms of ownership percentage of pre-existing investors like you.

This will happen if the company is continuously issuing new shares to be purchased by newer investors. Much like actual currencies, the value of shares will decrease if they're supplied in increased numbers. You should avoid companies that are constantly issuing new shares since you'll be suffering losses every time the company issues more of them.

Never Speculate

Since you're an investor, you should avoid any kind of speculation at all times. Speculation isn't something that characterizes an investor. It's something that gamblers do. There's a good reason why you should try to make decisions by examining the evidence rather than a hunch or the popular market sentiment.

Many times, the shares of good companies fall below the required threshold, and they fall into the category of penny stocks. These companies are hidden gems that can multiply your investments by a huge margin. However, in order to identify these companies, it's essential to first do your homework and look at the previous trajectory of any company whose stocks you're buying.

It's important to go by factual evidence since many companies go through a temporary phase of decline due to unforeseen circumstances like a global pandemic or a temporary trade embargo. However, these conditions won't last long, and if the company has strong fundamentals, then you can rest assured that it will bounce back. Be factual and find out the reasons behind everything that's happening in the stock market before you make a decision.

It's Not Raining Money

Many people are attracted to penny stocks because they have a pipe dream of becoming ultra-rich by just investing a small amount of money into these stocks. This is a common misconception that people often believe after they hear the occasional success story of someone who they don't even know personally.

However, you have to remember that these stories of underdogs making just one decision that flips their lives around are usually fictional. Even if they aren't fictional, the odds of you finding a miraculous stock are pretty low. Investing is about being intelligent rather than just being overly dependent on irrational things like luck. If you want to know what happens to those who just mindlessly follow the crowd, then just take a look at the dot com bubble, the various gold rushes throughout the world, or even the recent trend in cryptocurrencies where most of these new and overhyped crypto coins have just vanished into thin air.

If you develop this mindset of thinking before investing and not believing in anything other than facts and pieces of evidence, you can avoid the traps that most people fall for.

You'll be able to make decisions based on past data, which is much more likely to help you turn a profit rather than just investing in the latest fad. This mindset will ultimately help you out by forcing you to invest in the right penny stocks based on facts rather than the stocks that most other people choose based on their emotions alone.

Set Boundaries

It's very easy for a new investor to fall prey to the lower prices of penny stocks by underestimating the amount of money they spend. Since these penny stocks are priced so low, people often think that they can purchase an endless supply of these stocks without affecting their finances. This leads to the purchase of penny stocks that aren't nearly as fruitful as the ones you could've purchased if you were more rational and cautious.

However, you have to set a limit on the amount of money that you're willing to spend so that you can avoid poor decision-making. If you have a limited amount of money to spare, then you should be spending it very wisely and carefully, and this will help you avoid any investments that you might regret in the future.

Stay Updated

The number one piece of advice for any novice stock trader would be to stay up to date with any developments or changes in the market. This is essential because investors will often purchase a stock and then forget about it, which leads not only to loss of money but the loss of experience as well. This may seem like a tip that has been repeated over and over, but it's only because this tip is so important.

If you keep monitoring the current status of all your investments, then you'll be able to identify patterns and indicators that'll help you make better choices in the future. The only way to get good at trading is by engaging in trading and then learning from your mistakes. If you don't stay up to date on what's happening in the market and to your stocks, you'll never be able to learn and get better.

Evaluate All the Prospects

As we've discussed above, the companies that list their penny stocks are relatively small and have small market capitalization. However, a few companies often deviate from this general stereotype. You have to evaluate the entire company and its prospects before you invest your money because just looking at one or two parameters doesn't provide a comprehensive picture.

You have to evaluate if the management is reliable, whether or not the company is likely to issue more shares in the future, will there be any profits based on their current business model, is the company competitive in its segment, and much more.

If you can evaluate all these prospects and come up with a definitive answer, then you're good to go. You'll be able to make well-informed decisions by evaluating these facets, and these decisions will most likely be the best ones you can make.

Once you start to evaluate everything you come across, you'll also start seeing a trend that some sectors in an economy offer more penny stocks. These sectors will often offer penny stocks at the lowest prices and are worth taking a look at. The mining sector, for example, can offer you many opportunities to find a reputed company that trades in small amounts.

If you're willing to go above and beyond when conducting your analyses, research, and evaluations, you'll be able to surpass the competition. This may be one of the most important things that shouldn't be skipped if you want to find companies that'll be winners in the coming time.

The decision to pick the right penny stocks can be rather difficult for anyone, let alone a beginner. Quite often, even the most advanced traders find it challenging when they're just walking on the edge of profit or loss. It's only natural that a novice trader will be intimidated by the sheer complexity and variety present in the stock market.

Penny stock trading is even more complicated due to the higher number of companies that are listed under this category. You have to utilize every tool at your disposal to find out the hidden gems among the stocks that will be not very useful. If you can successfully utilize all the tools that are listed in this chapter, then your likelihood of striking gold increases hugely.

Just remember to be patient with yourself and start small. Everyone makes mistakes, and so will you. It's nothing to be frustrated about since making mistakes is a part of the learning process. Also, starting small will help you understand the market a lot better since you won't be very risk-averse with a small amount, and even if you lose some money, you won't mind starting from scratch. All in all, just be intelligent in the stock market, and you'll likely achieve success sooner or later.

Chapter 7: Trading Strategies

"I know where I'm getting out before I get in." - Bruce Kovner

To earn a profit by trading, you need to know the right time to buy stocks and the perfect time to let them go. A trader who doesn't let emotions dictate their trades has more chances of being successful. In addition to this, you must know and understand what you are investing in first. To be a good trader, you must be well-informed and well-versed in the performance of the stocks you have your eye on.

A trader must understand the patterns and be able to analyze the waves of the market. That said, success in stock trading is decided by the trading strategies that you employ.

The more effectively you establish and enforce your trading strategies, the bigger profits you'll earn trading stocks. Although every trade needs a customized approach, trading in penny stocks requires you to be all the more careful.

Since penny stocks have a very low price, you may find yourself being tempted to buy a big bulk. It is easy to forget the risks while expecting huge profits. As soon as the trader loses sight of the goal, they overlook the strategy that they decided before buying the penny stocks. This is what costs most penny stock traders their savings and even their livelihoods when the stocks suddenly crash. Many individuals who are just beginning in trading undermine the importance of a good trading strategy.

The potential gains and the affordability of penny stocks is the reason why many traders thrive on penny-stock trading. Most seasoned traders have established their trading strategies to double their profit on investments.

However, when you step into the trading market, you'll find a lot of people trying to manipulate your decisions and promote schemes that are more profitable for them. The dangers of trading are many, yet the profits make the risk worthwhile.

If you're also intrigued by the profitable prospects of trading, you may develop and follow a good trading strategy. In this informative and well-curated chapter, you'll discover the various trading strategies followed by expert traders.

In addition to this, you'll also learn about some risks that these strategies will help you prevent. By the end of this chapter, you'll have learned the most common and highly effective strategies to use for your trading business.

Without proper understanding, knowledge, and experience of the trade, making a business out of trading is like firing a shot in the dark. Even if one gets lucky, it's difficult to sustain profits in the long term. The penny stocks market is full of scammers, and it's not exactly news. If you aren't careful, being lured into a false scheme is more than possible. While penny-stock trading can earn you profit, it can also cost you. This is one more reason to follow good and proven trading strategies.

Having a good strategy will help you prevent and cut losses, ensuring that even when you lose, you'll have another chance to get back on your feet. This section lists the most effective strategies employed by experienced traders.

Stock Selection

Selecting a good penny stock determines your success or failure in trading. You need to scan for the best penny stocks by looking at their past patterns and performance. To solidify your chances of profit, you should filter the available options using some parameters.

These parameters may include a high market capital that can range between $50 and $300 million. In addition to this, you must ensure that the total volume traded is over 1 million every day. It is best to set the target price around 5% above the initial price. With that said, you must find a rising or falling pattern in the stock's simple moving average.

If you find a bullish hammer in the charts of the penny stock, it may indicate that the prices are bound to rise. On the other hand, if the simple moving average of the penny stock is falling, the chances are high that the prices will fall further. Most traders find it beneficial to cut their losses instead of putting those stocks on hold and waiting for them to rise in price. That said, it is best to select stocks that cost more than 50 cents a share. In addition to this, make sure the stock has a high number of shares traded every day. Otherwise, you'll risk getting stuck in an immovable position.

Set a Quantity Limit

Many traders have difficulty deciding the number of penny stocks they should buy. Quite often, stock-trading beginners end up buying far more shares than their risk-taking capacity. If the price of the stock falls, they end up losing money they can't afford. It not only hurts their financial health but also causes emotional turmoil.

With that said, some traders aren't able to judge the amount of money they can risk. They just can't make the best out of the available resources. It is therefore essential to calculate the amount of risk you can take. Consequently, you'll be able to figure out the number of stocks you can afford to buy without a huge risk.

To calculate the number of stocks you should buy, start by assessing the total amount in your trading account. After this, figure out the amount you can afford to risk. Once you've done that, divide the amount with the price of a rising stock. You'll get the number of shares you can risk buying. To understand it better, suppose you have $10,000 in your trading account. If you are okay with losing 20% of the total amount, it means you can afford to risk $2000 in the trade. Now, suppose the stock costs $1 a share. It means you can afford to buy 2000 shares with a 5:1 risk-reward factor. So, in this way, you'll have less trouble setting a limit on the quantity. When you know you can sustain the loss, you feel less stressed and more focused.

Utilizing Tips and Information

If you are into trading, you hear a lot of things on the street, on social media, and from other sources. While it is alright to ponder on the information and tips that you receive from other people, you should always conduct research yourself.

As you know by now, there are a lot of people who spread false information for their profit. This is the reason why you should not believe everything you hear. Quite often, even companies tend to spread rumors relating to expansions and rises in sales. In many cases, a staged rise in the price of a stock is followed by a sharp fall. Many inexperienced traders lose a lot of money in these situations.

As a rule of thumb, remember that you must be careful with the information you receive and know that you can't trust anyone. Unless you have solid proof along with supporting statistics, you must not go all in.

Companies may try to raise the price of the stock to earn a profit and stay in business. However, a lack of accurate data should be proof enough for you not to invest in this kind of penny stock. These schemes are nothing short of scams that only profit companies and their insiders. These people aim to manipulate the pricing of the stock. They use different means of promotions like spamming emails, press releases, and pump-and-dump schemes. Only when you are aware of manipulative promoters will you be able to distinguish credible information from Ponzi schemes.

Beware of Stock Promoters

The first change that you need to bring in your trading strategy is to become careful of the people that promote penny stocks. If you're a trader or even remotely interested in trading, you may have come across some spam emails, ads on social media, or text messages soliciting a penny stock. Many people love to prey on unaware trading beginners that have little to no knowledge of penny-stock trading.

The promoters take advantage of innocent people by luring them, touting success stories about companies, into investing in penny stocks. More often than not, the deceptive tactics work, and the investors end up losing a great deal of money.

The misleading promoters are experts in finding loopholes in the security regulations, which often gives them an advantage of being one step ahead. It is easy for these people to manipulate the penny-stock market. That said, sooner or later, these scammers get caught. However, you must always keep your guard up when you get a phone call from a penny-stock promoter out of the blue.

Perfect Your Timing

Trading in the penny stock market means that you need to have a good sense of when to enter and when to exit. If you sell too quickly, you may end up not utilizing the full potential of your trade. On the other hand, if you hold on for too long, you may risk losing a big chunk of your investment.

Knowing when to buy a stock and when to sell it comes after a lot of experience. However, if you stay up-to-date with the news and movement of the stocks you are planning to buy, you can make an informed decision without risking a lot of your money. In addition to this, when you buy a stock, you must decide on a time to sell it as well. Your timing plays a vital role in deciding whether you profit from a trade or not.

Many novice traders end up expecting a higher return is possible. The temptation of getting high profits in only a few days gets to the minds of many. The greed makes them miss the perfect time to sell. They fail to consider that the penny stock may be getting pumped up. In the penny stock market, what gets pumped also gets dumped.

You must make sure that you take any profits and let the stocks go once you've earned 20% profit. However, the trick to earn a huge profit is to sell fast but not to sell too short. Remember that penny stocks are very volatile and may take the wrong turn fast. Timing your entry into the market is important, but you should also set a limit on when you will exit the market.

Pay Attention to the Disclaimers

If you tend to rely on the information you find in newsletters and emails to plan your trading strategy, you must also go through the disclaimers very carefully. If you pay attention, you will realize that the newsletters and other sources have an ulterior motive behind promoting a company.

Most newsletters get a commission for displaying and pitching a stock on their channels. This strategy is used by companies to gain exposure and reach out to potential investors. However, the information and promises that you find in these newsletters and emails may not be 100% accurate.

This can be understood as a marketing strategy used by companies to raise the price of stocks.

Although it is acceptable to promote a company and its stocks, more often than not, the promises of returns displayed in the ads turn out to be false. You'd be surprised how many newsletters promote companies with a below-average return trend. You may feel tempted to buy stocks of a company that displays a good 52 week high.

However, there's a big difference between the stock making a 52-week high based on its earnings and the stocks getting pumped due to vigorous marketing.

To unearth the real reason behind a stock's success, you'll need to analyze the company's profit charts and compare them with the current price. This will help you evaluate whether the stocks are valued properly. In addition to this, the disclaimers present in the newsletters can also be indicative of a stock being overvalued.

If a stock is overvalued, the chances are its price will fall soon. Newsletters and emails rarely give the right information at the right time to sell a stock. If they do, it is often too late.

Don't Get Attached

Many full-time traders tend to get attached to a stock. Just because they got a tip from a trusted friend or a family member, they hold on to an unprofitable stock. Since their expectations are based on an unfounded tip, they usually end up losing money due to their attachment. It is important to leave your emotions aside when you step into the trading market. Apart from unprofitable stocks, many traders tend to stick to a strategy that doesn't benefit their style of trading.

Just because something works for a lot of people doesn't mean the same thing should work for everyone.

You need to adapt and evolve your strategy as you go. If your strategy doesn't help you earn a decent profit in a year, you must review it thoroughly and find the reasons behind this. Make sure that you do your research and establish a strategy that works best for you.

If something doesn't work, let it go and move on. If a stock isn't turning a profit after a long wait, maybe it's time to cut your losses and sell the shares. If a strategy isn't working for you, change it and try experimenting with other styles. Try until you discover a trading style that not only generates steady profits but also reduces the amount of risk.

To conclude this chapter on trading strategies, let us revise the key takeaways. The success of your trading business is greatly determined by your research, patience, and risk management. Having a good trading strategy can help you turn your investments into profits in a short amount of time. If there are flaws in your strategy or you fail to see obvious signs of an unprofitable stock, you may end up losing a lot of money trading stocks.

It is best to analyze the performance of a stock before investing any money. If you are trading penny stocks, you should pay attention to the simple moving average of the stock. If a stock displays a rising moving average, the chances are high that the price of the stock will increase. On the other hand, if the moving average of a stock is falling, the chances are high that the prices will also fall.

When you select a stock, do thorough research. While making an entry into the market or buying a particular stock, you must decide the limit at which you will sell the stock. Analyze the tips and information that you receive from your sources to confirm your predictions.

You need to determine the amount of risk you can afford. In addition to this, you must always beware of false promoters and pay attention to the disclaimers. With that said, you must not get attached to stock or a particular strategy.

If you feel like something isn't working out for you, you should reassess your methods and establish a new strategy based on your findings. A good trader knows when to buy a stock. But the best trader knows when to sell it.

Chapter 8: Fundamental Analysis

There are two main reasons why people are reluctant to invest in penny stocks. One is that the share prices of penny stocks are usually very volatile with a lot of daily variation.

The second is that since they are traded on less regulated OTC markets, which have fewer financial requirements, these companies don't always provide enough information for investors or analysts to make a calculated decision.

The Purpose of Fundamental Analysis

When you are looking to invest in stocks in general, and penny stocks in particular, it's always a good idea to have a look at what analysts are saying about that stock. When you look at the expert analysis, it can either be a fundamental analysis or a technical analysis.

The purpose of both analysis techniques is to evaluate whether or not a stock has been properly valued given the condition of the overall market. If the stock is valued differently from what the analysis suggests, this could be an investment opportunity or a red flag.

While fundamental analysis aims to give an investor a better idea of how fairly a share is priced in the market, it can also provide insight into the economic and financial health of the company. Using financial information provided by the company, the financial analysis determines how well the company is performing on its own and gives you an idea of whether or not you should invest in this company.

When analyzing the fair share price of a penny stock, analysts begin by studying the overall condition of the economy, the state of the specific industry the business is part of, and then the individual performance of that company. This way, a comprehensive fundamental analysis incorporates both macro and microeconomic factors to deduce a share price that can be deemed 'fair.'

If the calculated share price is higher than what the share is currently trading for, it is given an 'overweight' rating, meaning that the share is likely to increase in the future and it is a profitable investment option. On the other hand, if a share is given an 'underweight' rating, this means the share is currently trading for more than its market worth, and it is better to sell the share right now before the value drops.

As fundamental analysis can cover such a wide range of stats and measurements that are based on several different metrics, the findings can be divided into quantitative and qualitative measurements.

Quantitative vs. Qualitative

When we evaluate the overall health and position of a company, it can be evaluated both in terms of its fiscal measurement as well as in terms of intangible things such as the kind of business model it is using and the effectiveness of its policies. While it is important to keep an eye on the financials of a company, which will inform an investor on how profitable the company is and how economically sound it is, sometimes the intangible factors also play a big role in the overall performance.

The intangible aspects of a company can have a bigger influence on economic behavior and long-term growth than its physical assets.

Quantitative measurements are those that can easily be measured and those that have a numerical value attached to them. They are easy to compare and can be calculated in a well-defined manner. This will include things such as the company's profit, the value of its assets, the expenses that it is incurring, and the revenue that it's generating. Moreover, things such as the balance sheet, the income statement, and various other accounting statistics also fall under the quantitative category.

Qualitative measures will include things such as the value of the brand in terms of how well it is received by consumers, the kind of executive management the company has, the kind of patents, trademarks, or copyright technologies it company owns.,

The Basis of Qualitative Fundamental Analysis

When evaluating the qualitative features of a company for fundamental analysis, there are four key features that analysts typically look out for.

Competitive Advantage

Competitive advantage could be any tangible or intangible company. If you look at some of the biggest brand names in the world, they all have something unique to their product or service that their competitors are neither capable of replicating or even superseding. Due to this, they have a competitive advantage over the competition, which keeps customers coming back.

For investors, this means that this company is likely to keep paying them profits, and the share value is likely to continue rising in the future. Many companies that have this can easily turn into blue-chip companies after they have been paying consistent returns to investors for years on end.

Corporate Governance

Corporate governance covers all the rules, regulations, and procedures that the company adheres to. This will cover all the legal material that is stated in the company policy, the company bylaws, the internal policies, and corporate laws. Moreover, this will also be dictated by the laws and regulations which apply for that industry outside of the company itself and how well it implements these external rulings. Ideally, an investor wants to work with a company with laws that are transparent and ethical. That is usually an indicator that the company is efficient and fair in its dealings. The better these laws and regulations are, the easier it will be for an investor to get paid, understand where payment is coming from, and also how and why company performance is influencing the share price.

Management

This refers not only to the structure of the management and the overall hierarchy of the company but also to the actual people who are managing the company on a day-to-day basis. If you look at some of the best companies in the world, even though they have great products, proper management will always be what pushes them in the right direction during tough times.

Founders and even CEOs play the role of visionaries who guide the overall development of the company, while experienced managerial staff and an expert technical workforce make it possible for that vision to be brought to life. For some people, the management of a company is a pivotal measure of whether or not they should invest in it. If a company has managers with a proven track record of successful business endeavors, there is a high chance that they will be successful.

Business Model

While it's easy to say that a company sells shirts or manufactures electronics, it's still difficult to understand how exactly a company generates revenue. For instance, there could be a light manufacturer who has no innovative designs or technology, but they are extremely successful because they manufacture custom orders for clients with very large requirements.

On the other hand, another company producing lighting solutions in a quantity that is a fraction of what the mass manufacturer produces could be earning more profit since they have a patent for a unique technology.

The Basis of Quantitative Fundamental Analysis

Nearly any kind of financial statistic can potentially be used to analyze a company at a quantitative level. The most commonly used and trusted statistics are the companies' own financial statements.

Statement of Cash Flow

Cash flow statements depict a company's performance in a raw manner as they are all about keeping track of money as it flows through the ecosystem. Whereas other measurements of the company can, to some extent, be tampered with and calculated differently to produce a different result. It's not possible to change the way money is actually moving in and out of the company. There are three main activities that investors are interested in to learn the state of the cash flow.

Operating Cash Flow (OCF)

The amount of money generated from everyday business operations. This includes everything short-term, and that recurs on a daily basis. This also includes daily expenses and short-term expenses, giving a complete picture of where cash is coming from and where it is being spent.

Cash from Investing

This reflects all the cash that has been used to invest. This could include long-term assets or other investments that the company is making. If a company sells a part of the business or an associated company, a long-term asset, or some equipment, this is added to the CFI statement.

Cash from Financing

This will include any cash that is received from lenders and any cash that is paid out to borrowers. It also includes any expenses that were incurred in the lending or borrowing process and gives an exact account of how much cash was given or received and the incurred costs.

Balance Sheet

The balance sheet is like a snapshot of a business's financial position as it illustrates the 'balance' that the business is in at a particular point in time. A business is said to be balanced when

Total Assets = Total Liabilities + Equity

Assets can be described as everything tangible that the company owns that helps make them make money. Things such as inventory, machinery, property, and cash are all assets. Liabilities stem from debtors. This can include suppliers who have provided stock on credit or people who have rendered services and are yet to be paid. Equity is the money that the company has either received from investors or from a lending authority.

Income Statement

The income statement is what investors look at to find out how profitable a company is. At its core, this is a simple statement that illustrates how much money was generated in revenue, what the incurred expenses were during that time, and what the net profit is. Of course, it gets more detailed with larger companies as they have multiple streams of income, several expenses, and complex accounting procedures.

Quantitative Fundamental Analysis Systems

While you have plenty of information in the form of the various statements a company generates, these alone are not enough to evaluate whether a certain company is a good investment option. In order to analyze the real-time performance of a company, analysts use an assortment of ratios that depict the company's exact performance in certain areas. These ratios can then be compared to those of other companies to evaluate which is the best performer and which is the best option to invest in.

These are some of the most common ratios analysts use to evaluate performance; you can quite easily calculate these yourself for a company you are interested in if you have access to the appropriate data.

Performance Ratios

These ratios give a deeper insight into the profit a company is making. Rather than just quantifying it as an overall gross profit, through performance ratios, you can calculate the exact profit margin, the return on assets, the net profit margin, and the return on equity. For penny stocks, most of these figures will be very small.

However, what you should be looking for as an investor more than the size of the margins and returns, is consistent growth and positive numbers, month after month. Even though the profit margins may be low, if the company is surpassing cost or expenses and is achieving profitability every month or quarter, this is a promising sign.

Liquidity Ratios

Liquidity ratios illustrate how efficiently a company can pay back its lenders (shareholders and lending institutions) without having to acquire more debt. Penny stocks are notorious for low liquidity ratios meaning that they find it difficult to keep sales up to meet the payments they owe.

Ratios such as the quick ratio, cash ratio, and operating cash flow ratio show you how 'liquid' a company is and how easy or difficult it will be for the company to expand operations.

Leverage Ratios

Leverage ratios serve two purposes. First, they are used to understand how much of the working capital is being generated from debt (loans). This is important to consider since most companies will use a mixture of both debt and equity to fund their operations.

Secondly, these ratios show an investor how easy it is for a company to pay back its debt. Unlike liquidity ratios, leverage ratios are more focused on understanding how a company will deal with long-term debt rather than short-term debt. There are several types of leverage ratios, and they also help a person understand how a change in the company's output will influence its profitability. It isn't always necessary for profit to increase with output.

The main thing to keep an eye out for in leverage ratios is whether or not the profit margin on revenue is high enough for the company to easily pay back the interest rate on loans. Even if the company is making profits but is unable to meet loan payments, this can be troublesome for both lenders and investors.

A healthy company that is able to manage interest rates will be happy to acquire more debt and continue expansion. Contrary to popular belief having a small debt is not favorable as it could indicate that the company is struggling to expand its profit margins, and consequently, it is not risking taking on more debt.

There are various kinds of leverage ratios that can be used, but the most frequently used types of leverage ratios for penny stocks include the debt ratio and the interest coverage ratio.

While these are all important things you need to know about the fundamental analysis of stock options, it's also important to have a clear idea of what you want to achieve with your investment plan since a lot of these ratios and the various methods of analyzing stocks at a fundamental level depend entirely on what your approach is. One metric that is useful for someone else may not be that important to you even though you are both buying the same stock.

It is also important to know the specifications of the OTC marketplace through which you are trading penny stocks.

Most of these marketplaces do not have the same kind of requirements as larger exchanges. For this reason, a lot of the companies that are traded through OTC markets won't publish the necessary documentation that is required for this kind of analysis. This is where you become limited in how you are able to weigh out penny stock options because sufficient data is not always available.

However, penny stocks can still be manageable if you choose your marketplace wisely and work only with OTCs that require firms to publish information regularly. This significantly reduces the chances of you investing in a company that only looks good on the stock exchange.

Investing in such companies can not only lead to a loss, but it can be very difficult to get rid of these shares when you want to sell. Other people may not be interested in buying these shares

Chapter 9: Technical Analysis

Where fundamental analysis goes in-depth on why and how a company or a specific stock will be a good investment, technical analysis analyzes an investment on the same basis using price evaluation techniques.

People who prefer Technical Analysis (TA) are of the opinion that the current market price is already a good representation of what people think about it. They assume that the people who are trading the stock at the current market price have already associated a fair price with the stock and that the subsequent variations that occur are a reflection of their shifting opinion on the stock.

For this reason, they believe, as an investor, if we can just evaluate the price, this is enough to evaluate whether we should or shouldn't invest in a stock.

Keeping this in mind, FA is more frequently used by investors who are looking to gain value in the long term. They are less interested in short-term gains through trading and are banking more on the fact that since the company is performing well, the share price is going to increase in the long term. They invest in small companies that are cheap today but will be on the blue-chip spectrum tomorrow.

TA traders, on the other hand, are more interested in short-term benefits. They are looking for a stock that offers quick high returns. Ideally, through TA, they will be able to identify what the highs and lows of a stock are, and they will try to buy low and sell high.

For this reason, TA as a whole is more suited to penny stocks and other stock options that are highly volatile yet also liquid. You wouldn't want to be stuck with a stock that can bring you a profit, but you can't sell it. Applying TA to a stock that is relatively slow-growing and has a very small variation in price won't be very valuable unless you are investing very large amounts of money.

When investing using both TA and FA, there are different approaches you can take, and either one can work for both types of analysis depending on how you invest.

Analysis Styles

Top Down

When you analyze using the top-down approach, you will start from a macroeconomic perspective and work your way downwards. You would consider the overall state of the economy, then the specific conditions of the industry within that economy, and then the state of certain companies within that industry.

Depending on whether you are looking for short-term or long-term gains, you may want to delve into industries that are highly volatile or those that are growing at very slow rates but which are showing a consistent upward trend.

Bottom-Up

The bottom-up approach is the complete opposite of the former. In this approach, the main focus is the price of the stock itself and the behavior of this price during a given time frame. Ideally, an investor using the bottom-up strategy will be looking for a stock that is in a downward trend.

By studying the overall trend of the stock, they will know when the price reaches a low point, and that will be their entry point. Then when the stock starts to ascend, they will exit near the peak, taking the profits gained during the upwards trend.

Time Frames

When investors are using TA to understand the behavior of a stock, the most important thing to consider is the time frame. The TA school of thought is based on the fact that a certain stock will replicate its price behavior in the future.

However, depending on the time frame, this could mean that a stock will replicate its behavior in the next five minutes based on the behavior that it demonstrated in the past five minutes, or what it will do in the next year depending on what it did last year.

When you are studying the price chart of a stock, you can choose whatever time frame suits your needs. However, the most commonly used time frames are usually 5 minutes, 15 minutes, one hour, four hours, and daily charts.

The width of the time frame that you select will depend entirely on the kind of trading that you want to do and partially on the kind of stock you are trading. People who are leaning towards intra-day trading will prefer shorter price charts, whereas those looking for more long-term investment will rely more on longer price charts.

Technical Indicators

Traders who use TA information rely on a vast array of price indicators to show them how the stock is performing and how it could potentially perform in the future. Using this price behavior information, investors and traders make their decisions. These are some of the most frequently used indicators as they cover a good amount of the information a trader needs.

Moving Averages

Rather than having to constantly look at the highs and lows of security, traders choose to look at moving price averages that even out the overall price changes in security. This average price could represent changes in any given time frame. Some may choose to look at the moving price average of five minutes, five hours, or even five months.

A commonly used price average is a 50-day price average. Some traders also choose to use more than one average, so they may be looking at the 50 days, 100 days, and 200-day moving average simultaneously.

When a short-term moving average rises above a long-term moving average, the stock is said to be in upward momentum. Opposite to this, when a short-term moving average moves lower than a long-term moving average, the stock is said to be in downward momentum.

Moving averages can also be further classified into exponential moving averages and simple moving averages.

A simple moving average is easily calculated by adding up the highest and lowest prices of a stock and then dividing that by the number of total averages. The main difference between a simple and exponential moving average is that the exponential moving averages give more weightage to recent price changes.

Pivot Points

Pivot points are especially useful for swing traders. They allow a trader to see where a stock price maxes out or bottoms out. It also helps identify various support points and resistance points. This information is helpful when a trader is looking for an entry point or an exit point, so they can make their move at an optimal price. It also gives them a price bracket within which they can carry out trades. However, prices are also known to exhibit unusual behavior, and they do this when they go higher or lower than their pivot points as well as their defined support and resistance points, and this behavior is known as a 'breakout.'

Pivot points are usually calculated on a daily basis using the previous day's highs, lows, opening, and closing points.

Fibonacci Levels - Retracements and Extensions

The Fibonacci levels, or ratios, are widely used to understand both the entry points for a stock and its profit targets. It gives investors an exact amount that they aim to either purchase at or sell out at. Fibonacci levels are in the form of ratios, such as 0.24, 0.38, .etc., but are more commonly used in corresponding percentage values, 24%, 38%, etc.

These are not difficult to use, and many free tools will automatically calculate these for you for any given stock. These ratios are used for a variety of purposes, but most frequently, they are employed to understand retracements and extensions. Retracements tell us about the correction a stock is likely to make after it has undergone a sustained period of upward or downward movement.

By calculating the retracement points, you can find safe spots to either enter or exit.

The way a retracement is calculated is, say, a stock price starts at $20 and moves all the way up to $50; that's a $30 increase. Investors will want to know at which price the market will find support and then continue to move upwards. If you are estimating that the price will find support after a 38% retracement, you will be looking to buy the stock at $41, as 38% of 30 is 9, so $50-$9=$41.

On the other hand, now that you have bought a share at the retraced price, you also want to know when you should sell this stock; for this, you will need to calculate the extension price.

The Fibonacci extensions are measured in increments similar to the retracements but only 100% higher, so they are 126%, 138%, etc. Also, these are measured from the lowest point of the retraced price, so when you buy at $41, and that was the lowest retracement, you will calculate 126% of $41. That would look like - $41 + (30x1.26) = $78.8, so ideally, you should be selling at $78.

These are extremely popular methods to use when trading, and if you study the price movements of a different stock option, you will notice that their behavior is closely aligned to these ratios. This is not because these are magic ratios, but there are so many traders using these numbers that the overall market trend is reflected in these ratios.

This makes it more possible to understand future moves of the stock, which can help you even if you aren't using these ratios directly.

How You Can Use Technical Analysis

The way you can use TA and even FA will depend heavily on what your end goals are and how you are investing. Are you looking to make a short-term profit? Are you trying to put your savings in a stock that will grow and benefit you near retirement? Do you want to invest in a slow-growing industry? All of these things will determine how you use the two types of analyses.

Strategy

Overall, strategies can be broadly categorized into passive and active strategies. As the names imply, people using passive strategies will not be making a lot of trades, taking a passive approach, and letting their investments grow.

Active strategies are what regular traders use. They don't mind transaction fees as they believe they will soon make a profit. There are a few types of strategies that can be used for both short-term and long-term gain.

Growth Investing

This is a strategy mostly employed by people looking for long-term growth and who want to build the value of their portfolio. They invest in companies that they believe will grow in value in the long term, possibly ten years or more. They buy today so that they can profit from it several years down the line. This is also used by short-term investors when they choose to invest in a company that they believe will achieve exponential growth in a year or two. They will hold stocks either for a certain time or until they reach a certain value and then sell.

Income Investing

This is a strategy adopted by investors who are looking to invest in something that will provide an income for them. They are less focused on the actual value of the stock or security and more on the kind of dividend or fixed interest that it pays.

Contrarian Investing

This is a strategy in which investors are constantly on the lookout for when the market takes a downturn. They are interested in buying stocks at the lowest price possible and then holding them until they reach peak value. In the short term, they may be looking for downturns caused by the behavior of the market, while in the long run, events such as war and natural disasters can cause stock prices to plummet.

The recovery period will also depend on what the cause of the downturn is. When the price reaches its peak, they cash out. However, it's important to note that not all stocks that plummet in price return to market price or reach their peak. Some stocks never return to acceptable or even profitable prices.

Swing Trading

This is the most used trading style by people who rely heavily on TA. This is all about watching the price and looking for trends as the price 'swings' from highs to lows. They aim to purchase a stock when they believe it has swung to a low and will now swing back to a high. Swing trading can be used for both long-term and short-term approaches.

The duration of the swing is also used to analyze the level of support or resistance a stock has. Traders will also monitor momentum and the overall trend to understand whether future swings will occur at higher or lower price points.

Choose an Investment Type

With your strategy in mind and your style of analysis at hand, you need to find an investment option with a style that suits your needs. For day-traders and those looking to earn quick returns, the ideal stock will be volatile and have a reasonably predictable life cycle. Those who are in it for the long run will be inclined to go for more stable options that exhibit consistency in their patterns. Longer, general trends will be the focus.

Brokers

For every kind of investor, there is a broker. Whether this is in terms of the security that you want to trade or the trading style that you want to adopt, you will find a broker that specializes in each possible kind of trading.

Not only will they be experienced in the market and security that you are interested in, but their entire service will be focused on their expertise. If you are looking to trade in penny stocks, even if you have the necessary knowledge, you will still need someone that offers the appropriate account type and has the kind of services that will make penny stock trading profitable.

Using the wrong kind of account could prove to be so expensive and actually prevent you from making a good profit if any at all.

Monitor Performance

If you are trading penny stocks, then monitoring performance is crucial. Even for other forms of securities that are just as volatile, a constant eye on the market is vital if you want to make unexpected profits and save yourself random losses.

Moreover, keeping a close eye on the behavior of your stock will help you understand the overall trend and make it easier to act in the future. It's also a good idea to record this information so you have solid statistics that you can refer to whenever you need.

Improve Analysis

While your own knowledge and the input from your broker are great sources of information, the more you know, the better your trades can be. Today traders have access to a plethora of resources that they can access at the click of a button.

While it can be time-consuming to absorb all this information, investing in analysis software and apps is also a great idea. These resources can also lower the workload for you as an investor. Many apps and software give you the option to set price limits, sell or buy options and even the ability to automate your entire trade process.

Chapter 10: Risk Management

Beginners in the penny stock trading market often lose themselves in researching various trading methods, completely disregarding the risks these stocks can represent. As penny stocks are shares that trade for less than $1 per share, they are often considered low-risk investments.

However, in some cases, even trading with penny stock trading can carry huge risks, especially for inexperienced investors. Running into a scam or trading more than you can afford could put you into a dire financial situation or at least make it impossible for you to trade again in the near future.

For this reason, this chapter is dedicated to the basics of risk management and common risks that you can come across.

Risk management is a skill that most successful traders possess. It can help you stay in the trading game for as long as possible. It's not one quick fix that can eliminate your mistakes. It's a series of basic steps you take during trading.

They serve the purpose of protecting your money when you're just starting out. This way, you are able to earn more money for years to come. Even if you make some minor mistakes at the beginning of your learning process, you will still be able to continue trading. As long as you can keep yourself from falling prey to huge scams and you learn how to stay consistent, you will gain tons of experience and hopefully reach your goals. Experience you gain from penny stock trading can be easily translated into other types of trading. One of the key factors in risk management is keeping your focus on the right things.

For example, it can teach you to not dwell on past losses and focus on what you can gain in the future instead. After all, no strategy can help you become successful in penny stock trading if your own negative mindset is bringing you down. Plus, focusing on losses only brings more losses.

Even if they aren't high in value, little by little, your losses can hurt your trading capability in a big way. So, aside from perfecting your trading strategies and maximizing your gains, you will need to focus on minimizing your losses.

Basics of Risk Management in Penny Stock Trading

Do Your Research

The importance of research has been discussed earlier in this book so, in this section, we'll focus on its role in risk management. A proper investigation of various penny stock trading techniques will allow you to determine your own expectations.

When doing that, keep in mind that these are low-value shares, and it usually takes years to reach your goals. Figuring out your main interests is a good start, but make sure they will bring you profit in a realistic time frame.

Don't Rely on Trading Only

Again, penny stock trading is a long-term process, and you can't expect any financial gains - at least not in the beginning. For this reason, it's recommended you do this only if you have a steady income or some sort of financial security.

Much later, you may earn enough from your stocks to live off of. As a beginner, you will definitely need to have an income or some money set aside. Even if you are careful and don't invest too much money, you can still run into scams and lose what you invested. You still have bills to pay, so don't rush into this, thinking you will quickly turn a profit.

Only Invest Money You Can Afford to Lose

Some trading types, like OTC, are riskier than others, and it's made worse by the possibility of overextensions. For this reason, if the stock crashes, being over the line can carry terrible financial consequences.

And if you have invested money you need for other purposes, you will lose even more. To avoid this, it's recommended to have a budget only for trading purposes and keep it separate from your monthly budget. Only after you are sure you can cover everything in that budget and have some leftover money should you consider investing or trading. In the beginning, this amount shouldn't be more than 2% of your paycheck, and even later on, it should never surpass 10%. On top of this, you should add a certain percentage for risk modulation, so even if you lose some money, you will still be financially okay.

Don't Rush with Investments

Some deals are more tempting than others, but you should avoid rushing into any of them. Make sure you put enough time into the complete evaluation of the trade. Consider this a lesson in patience and self-discipline.

Yes, it's understandable if you want to earn more money by investing or trading. However, as a beginner, this won't be possible for you right away. Instead, if you're not careful, you may run into a scam.

Even if you have had some success with penny stocks before, this should never be a guarantee that you'll get the same results. So, be smart by being vigilant and aiming to gain experience along the way.

Learn When to Cut Your Losses

Unfortunately, a large number of traders suffer losses at the beginning of their careers. This is why it's crucial to follow up with your investment. As soon as you notice your stock dropping, you should cut your losses before you lose too much.

Losing over 20% could mean you won't have enough money to invest in a more lucrative trade in the near future. And this can happen even with your most promising trades, so you should always be prepared for unexpected scenarios.

Have a tailored stop percentage for each of your stocks so you can react in time in the worst-case scenario. Additionally, you will need to accept that these setbacks are normal. You should not be discouraged.

Consider Whether the Stock Is Worth The Risk

Investing or trading in any stock is risky, and there is no getting around that fact. Some stocks are more worthy of risking your hard-earned money than others, and it will be up to you to figure out which is which. Even though they have low values, these penny stocks belong to companies that are in less than ideal financial situations.

You will have to evaluate whether they can be saved or not, which will determine if they are worth the investment. Every successful trader took years to learn how to do this, so it's no big deal if you slip up at the beginning. With time, you will learn how to recognize the stock that will make taking the risk and waiting for it to improve well worth it.

What to Be Aware of

During your research, you may have come across some unusual trading strategies, which could make you question their validity. Fortunately, not all of them are high risk. However, before jumping into any of them, it's still recommended to keep an eye on some of these and do more detailed risk evaluations. No matter how tempting some of these opportunities are, they are never worth the risk of losing your money.

Here are some of the most common scams you may encounter while trading with penny stocks:

Pump and Dumps: This is a pretty simple scam. Someone will try to oversell the idea that a company is worth it. Even though these are virtually unknown businesses, the scammer will try to convince you otherwise. By buying the shares of these companies, you will only raise their value. That is exactly what they are after.

Once they are satisfied with the price, they will dump the stock and get away, leaving you without your money and with useless stock. These scammers work with inflated promotions, so they are easy to recognize if you are vigilant enough.

Short-and-Distort Scams: Being the opposite of the previous one, these scams rely on deliberately lowering the value of the shares using any means possible. Before that, they had already borrowed shares from an investor and sold them immediately after. When the value of the stock drops, these short sellers buy them back at a much lower price. Then the scammers will return the shares to the investor, but they will keep the money they have earned during the process. If you invest in a stock like this, you will be guaranteed to lose a considerable amount of money.

Reverse Merger Illusions: It's not uncommon for a private company to merge with a public one. Companies in dire financial situations often do this, so when they are selling their stock, they can avoid the expenses of traditional listings.

Unfortunately, this means that the value of the public company's shares will add to the value of the private business's stocks, so investors will pay a higher price for them. After all, if a business has higher earnings, this automatically raises the prices of its stock. Fortunately, a merger should always be presented in the data you get from the company you are thinking of investing in.

Mining Scams: Probably the oldest scams that exist are the ones related to companies involved in the oil, precious metal, or gem business. As these fields present an opportunity for a quick gain, it's easy for scammers to find someone interested in investing in them. The problem is many of these companies use false advertising.

They either don't possess enough value to be explored, or they haven't discovered the source of the product they are advertising at all. They only make you think they do just so they can take your money.

The Guru Deceptions: The number of "experts" promising to teach you how to trade in penny stocks in exchange for a small compensation is rising rapidly. And the reason for that is a simple one. It works.

Beginner traders often look for any information on making successful investments, and they often fall victim to false advertisements. These promotions often urge you to invest in deals that are too good to be true. Or, they will pitch you a technique that's supposed to work with all your future penny stock trades. Either way, they are only looking for a quick payout, and they give nothing in return.

The No Net Sales: Some scammers will offer you very promising stock deals and even throw in the fact that there is a considerable demand for these shares. This way, they will urge you to close the deal much faster and disregard taking the necessary safety precautions.

However, there will be a catch. If you want to make money on them, you can't sell the stock for a certain amount of time. Of course, this is another lie the seller is telling the investor, and it only serves the purpose of them getting away with their scam for a longer period of time.

Offshore Investments: Companies registered in foreign countries usually aren't subjected to the same rules as businesses operating in your country. They aren't obligated to reveal the exact number of their shares all the time, and scammers love to take advantage of this. By buying their stock at a low value and selling the shares to investors at much higher prices, the scammers can deflate the value of the stock. They will earn a lot of money on the trade, while you, the investor, will not only not gain any income, but you are lucky if you actually don't lose any money.

How to Avoid Being Scammed

Scammers are constantly developing new techniques, and there isn't a sure way to avoid them. With that being said, there are some steps you can take so you won't easily fall into their traps, or at least minimize your losses in case you become a victim of a scam. The first thing you can do is learn how to distinguish equity research from stock promotions.

Genuine researchers are not compensated for their work in stock. If during an evaluation you see that the writer did get paid, this is a scam. The researchers of the trader are nothing more than talented writers hired to promote the stock with detailed and often misrepresented facts and should be avoided at all costs.

Apart from the stock itself, you should also look at the management behind it. Get a report of every key person in the trading company you are considering for your next trade. Pay particular attention to whether they were involved in any trading before and how successful their past deals were. If more than one person from the same company has notable failures, or even worse, scams on their record, you shouldn't go into business with them.

While you are taking a close look at the company, make sure you also evaluate its overall financial situation. Due to legal reasons, you probably won't find out every little detail, but you could still use whatever information you can get.

The more data the company discloses to you, the more likely they are being transparent. This is particularly important in high-risk OTC stocks, where most scams usually happen. If they don't provide you with any financial reports, it could mean that they are hiding something.

Whether it's for the lack of data or unsatisfactory values, you have every right to pass on whatever deal they are offering. And this is true for both the company and the stock. The more data you possess on both, the more confident you can be.

And finally, you should evaluate whether investing in the stock will bring you the desired profit in a reasonable amount of time. To do that, look at the company's business plan and consider how viable it is. It should be set at an attainable level, and more importantly, covered financially.

If you see that the company may not have the funds to cover their plans or hasn't worked out every crucial detail, you should stay away from them. Investing in stocks like this is a recipe for disaster.

Even after you have learned how to manage risks in penny stock trading, you should stick to some basic rules.

Not limiting yourself to buying only one type of stock constantly is a good idea. And no matter how profitable the shares are, selling them when the time comes is one of the most important things you can do. Knowing when to sell or buy a particular stock is also a valuable skill to possess, as this will allow you to earn more money with each trade you make.

Chapter 11 Mistakes Investors Make

When it comes to trading and investing, you must understand that mistakes are part of the learning process. If you are a newbie to trading penny stocks, you should know that a lot of different things can go wrong.

Even experienced traders can and will make mistakes sooner or later. This chapter outlines the common mistakes that traders often make and provides some tips on how to avoid them.

Finding the Right Broker

The first step that you should take before you start trading is finding the right broker. There are several brokers that you can consider, but the challenge lies in choosing the right one. The broker you choose will significantly impact your future in trading. Before you open an account, you must go through the trading platform offered by your preferred broker to see if it is user-friendly.

You should understand the terms and conditions before signing up for your account. Brokers charge service fees, and they also offer different payment methods. Therefore, you must carefully select a broker that offers services that suit your needs. It is a good idea to practice using a demo account before beginning actual trading. Many brokers offer free demo accounts that are designed to help beginner traders get a better feel of the platform. A demo account is a replica of the real account that you will use for real trading.

Lack of Trading Plan

Many beginner traders make the mistake of starting out without a trading plan. This is risky since you do not have any goals or objectives, and your trade will be directionless.

If you are a newbie to penny stock trading, you should avoid the folly of buying or selling stocks without a plan. It is critical to have a well-defined trading plan that outlines your entry and exit points.

Your trading plan should also state the amount of capital that you wish to invest as well as the maximum loss that you are willing to take. The other error that you should avoid is deviating from your written plan, hoping to get lucky and making a quick turnaround. The danger of trading without a plan is that you are likely to experience heavy losses.

Choose a Trading Strategy

Many people make a fatal penny stock trading mistake by just following success stories of other traders and deciding to randomly jump in and start trading. Penny stock trading does not operate like that.

You must have a viable strategy that will guide you every step of the way. You also need to take some time to get training to master the basic techniques that will help you build a solid foundation.

To select the right strategy, you should be willing to learn different things. You must give yourself time to discover new things and develop a style that can make you a formidable trader in the long run. Learning is an ongoing process where you should show some willingness to do your own research on investments and potential trades.

You should know that penny stocks are not regulated like the companies that operate on national exchanges. The other important element is that you must have an interest in reading to gain insight into different factors that can affect the economy. Economic conditions outside the world of trading can and will have an impact on stock trading.

Respect Your Instincts

Unfortunately, many penny stock promoters cannot tell you the truth about these facts since their promotions are usually self-serving. These people will tell you that your investment is great, yet they are primarily concerned about their business.

When you choose to listen to outside advice, make sure you do your research to make an informed decision. Additionally, you should also respect your intuition when you are about to invest.

You do not necessarily need to be a prophet or rocket scientist to invest in a winning deal. If you get proper training in penny stock trading, your gut feeling or instinct can be very powerful since it can help you make a wise decision.

When you doubt something, it is better to walk away than regret it later. Make sure you listen to your inner voice before you start trading. Your instincts can give you proper guidance if you follow them.

However, the other mistake that can affect your trading is that you may be too cautious. You should have the courage to take the risk if you decide to venture into trading. Trading penny stocks requires you to have a high-risk tolerance. When you are a trader, you must understand that no gain comes without risk. You will realize that some risks come with greater rewards.

Ignoring Risks

While it is true that some risks offer better rewards, the opposite may be true when trading stocks. Stock markets are characterized by high risks that include factors like market volatility which means that stock prices are never steady. Some traders cannot comprehend the ups and downs that characterize stock trading. If you cannot manage risk, it is essential to stay away from the volatile shares offered by different companies.

Penny stock trading is not about securing a steady income that comes with fixed interests. Just like gambling, investing in stocks does not guarantee revenue generation. Losses are inevitable.

To avoid risks as much as possible, you must use the stop-loss order option that is designed to prevent your investment from going through in the event of adverse stock performance.

The stop-loss order automatically halts trade once you reach your cap. It is also vital to learn other tricks that you can implement to mitigate risks and learn how the market functions. If you get an understanding of how the market functions, you will gain more confidence, and you will take more chances when you trade.

Have a Strong Routine

Not having a strong routine is another big mistake that you can make when trading penny stocks. Trading involves the repetition of the same activity over and over again. This will help you form good habits and routines. When you have a clear routine, you can easily notice when things are going well and when something is not right. You will be in a better position to make necessary adjustments to your trades if you keep a detailed diary.

It takes great effort and discipline to succeed in penny stock trading. If you are reluctant and you cannot dedicate time to grow your money, then you may not be quite ready for this. You must create a watch list that will help you study patterns in your stocks. Experience is the best teacher in whatever you do, but you must tread carefully. Find as many ways as possible to gain experience without risking your money. Simulations and trading demos are a great way to do that risk-free.

Not Working with a Mentor

Many people fail in penny stock trading because they think they know everything and that they are above asking questions. Trading is tricky, as many people would imagine. It is a big mistake to start trading without proper guidance. If you are concerned about success in your trades, you should seek guidance from an experienced mentor.

You can join a network of traders to learn different things from them. The good thing about mentorship is that you will not learn the hard way. You have the ability to soak up years of experience and, most importantly, to learn from the mistakes and mishaps of other people.

You can access invaluable information and advice based on experience from your mentor. Working with someone with knowledge of penny stock trading can also go a long way in boosting your confidence. A mentor can introduce you to helpful tips and other resources that can improve your trade.

Avoid Unfounded Tips

You must work with a reliable mentor and avoid unfounded tips from promoters of different types of stocks. Commonly, you can hear your peers talking glowingly about specific trades, and you may be tempted to try them. However, it can be a terrible mistake if you blindly follow trade with a promise of killer earnings. While it may be true that the chances of better earnings will be high, you should not rush.

Investment professionals on different channels are other people who often provide unfounded tips to investors. These stocks that are often touted as must-buys will turn out to be a hoax meant to attract buyers. Buying stocks based on media hype is more like speculative gambling. You do not necessarily need to jump on the stock tip. It is vital to check the source of the tip that grabs your attention. You must do your homework first so that you know what you are buying.

Bear in Mind Position Sizes

Some people make the mistake of failing to keep position size in mind when they begin trading. Trading position sizes that are too big can be problematic since they may risk your investment when you pay more attention to one particular kind of trade. It is usually a good idea to start with a small stake and gradually increase as you learn the ropes. Unless you are prepared to start over again, you must not risk your account on a single trade. Utilize good risk management practices and fair judgment when you trade.

What you wish for does not affect the market, so you must be realistic and avoid risking all your money in one trade. It is crucial to test your strategies for trading using small portion sizes. These smaller portion sizes will allow you to gauge your winning rate. You can refine your trading strategy and gradually increase the portion size as you familiarize yourself with market trends.

Chasing after Performance

Some traders make the mistake of chasing after performance by trying to follow other traders' footsteps. While there is nothing inherently bad about learning from observing other experienced traders, you should not copy everything they do.

You must design your own trading strategies and select asset classes that are based on current performance reports. Some people end up making bad investments because they followed trades that worked well for others.

If you see a certain asset class or fund doing extremely well, it may be too late to jump on the bandwagon since the tide can turn at any time. Those who are enjoying the current performance have made decisions months or even years ago. The challenge you may face is that the cycle of great performance in the market might be nearing its end, and you may lose out. Trading is not an overnight event but a long process that requires careful planning. You need to plan your investment and understand that something that works for someone else might not work for you.

Treat Trading as a Business

Many people fail to realize their goals because they view penny stock trading as a hobby instead of a business. There is no easy way to riches when you decide to venture into trading. This type of overconfidence can pose a threat to some traders who may become complacent and reckless. Most traders who are overconfident perform badly in their trades. To increase your chances of success, you must treat trading as a full-time job, not a hobby.

Learn to Accept Losses

A successful trader can quickly study the trend of the stock market and quickly make an informed decision. For instance, if you realize that the trade is not working out in your favor, you can take a break and revisit your strategy. Alternatively, you can consider moving on to another trade idea instead of sticking with a hopeless trade.

When it becomes apparent that there is no hope of recouping the loss, there is no reason to hold on to a losing position. You may risk losing more trading capital.

Similarly, you must also teach yourself to accept losses. Investors are human too, and they are prone to make mistakes that can be costly. Some investors fail to acknowledge that they can make mistakes. If your long-term investment hits a brick wall and turns out to be a bad deal, you should learn to accept it and move on. You should also avoid situations where your emotions drive you. This is one of the worst mistakes that you can ever make. Never hold on to a losing investment out of hope, blind faith or loyalty. You can also be tempted to purchase more shares if you realize that the stock is currently cheaper. This can be suicidal since the move can backfire, and you end up experiencing heavy losses.

Do not Underestimate Your Abilities

Many people engaged in penny stock trading make the mistake of giving up too early. However, real players soldier on until they achieve their desired goals. You may feel the urge to give up trading, but this is a big mistake since you can ruin your chances of success. Stock trading is like gambling, and it may not be easy to predict the outcome.

When you accept that penny stock trading comes with inevitable risks, then there is no reason why you should decide to give up before earning a profit. Self-confidence is vital if you want to master the art of trading.

Many people tend to underestimate their abilities when it comes to trading due to fear of the unknown. They believe that stock markets are complicated, and they are reserved for experienced investors. Unfortunately, this myth has no basis since professional finance managers in large companies also underperform when it comes to stock trading. What you need to do is to give yourself time to research and learn different things about stock markets. This can go a long way toward helping you equip yourself with the right knowledge to manage your growing portfolio and make informed decisions. You need to be rational and apply some common sense if you want to succeed in penny stock trading.

Bottom Line

Penny stock trading can be lucrative if you have sound investment strategies. However, many people tend to make several mistakes that are mainly influenced by elements like fear of the unknown.

When you decide to join the penny stock market, never underestimate your potential since you can overcome all the challenges and make your investment pay off. You must utilize rational investment strategies that you can stick with and feel comfortable with.

Conclusion

"The hard work in trading comes in the preparation. The actual process of trading, however, should be effortless." - Jack Schwager

This book's aim is to make you more knowledgeable about penny stock trading. If you've reached the end of this informative book, you have probably learned a great deal to help propel your trading journey in a profitable direction. As a beginner in penny stock trading, it is vital to get your facts right and understand the fundamentals of stock trading. The stronger your base, the easier your trading business will be.

In this highly descriptive book, you learned everything there is to know about stocks. You learned why you always need to be smart and vigilant when trading stocks. Now, it'll be a lot easier for you to understand and correctly use the most common trading terminologies.

The first chapter of this book had a dedicated section to help you understand how the New York Stock Exchange (NYSE) and National Association of Securities Dealers Automated Quotations (NASDAQ) operate and their role in trading. We discussed the rise and fall in the prices of stocks and the subsequent patterns that are often called the bull and bear patterns. Apart from these concepts, we also discussed the method of short-selling, where a seller sells a stock they don't own.

In the second chapter of this comprehensive guide, you learned that penny stocks are those that have a very low market capitalization and can be traded at a really low price. In addition to being mainly illiquid, penny stocks are usually listed on smaller exchanges.

The second chapter discussed and covered everything there is to know about penny stocks. We also explained the process of how the securities of companies that are not listed on any formal exchange are traded. Also known as over-the-counter (OTC) stocks, these stocks help companies raise money through the selling of stock. By the end of chapter 2, the volatility of penny stocks became clearer to imagine.

The third chapter of this book walked you through different ways to find the right broker for your trading account. It is essential to remember that a broker can have a great impact on your trading experience. You must research the background and track record of the broker before agreeing to hand over your trading account.

At the start of the next chapter, you learned about the things one must consider before buying stocks. The chapter also helped you understand what risk money is and how to use it. As this chapter concluded, we explained the importance of being attentive to the various trends of the stock market. This chapter also warned you about the mindset you should avoid when trading penny stocks.

The fifth chapter helped you explore the process of developing a strategy. You learned how our wants, needs, resources, personality types, and preferences could help shape a perfect and profitable trading strategy. In addition to this, we pondered over the importance of doing research and understood how some external factors affect the stock exchange market.

We also showed you how trading imbalances, company growth, industry changes, and media act as catalysts of certain market behaviors. Another key takeaway from this chapter was the importance of learning market behavior by knowing the company or industry and learning chart patterns.

In the following chapters, we explored the numerous ways of picking the right penny stock. In addition, we also surfed through various tips and important points to remember while making a trading strategy. We shed light on the most efficient strategies to help you improve your trading game.

The eighth chapter was dedicated to the purpose of fundamental analysis in penny stock trading. We explained the difference between qualitative and quantitative models. We discovered the key features that analysts use when evaluating the qualitative features of a company, namely, competitive advantage, corporate governance, management, and business model. We explained how cash flow, balance sheets, and income statements become the basis of fundamental quantitative analysis. We also discussed the most common ratios used by analysts to evaluate performance, such as performance ratios, liquidity ratios, and leverage ratios.

In the final few chapters of this book, you learned all about technical analysis. The ninth chapter covered the importance of technical analysis and why it is used in the penny stock market. With that said, we went over the basics of risk management in trading. It is essential for you to do your research and not rely on trading only.

It is wise to only invest money you can afford to lose. You must not rush with investments. Most importantly, you should learn when to cut your losses and consider whether the stock is worth the risk.

This factual trading guide enlightened us with some of the most common mistakes made by investors. A lack of a trading plan, inefficient trading strategy, and ignorance of risks can lead you to huge and irreversible losses. It is best to avoid chasing mindlessly after stocks or strategies that have worked for others. You must treat trading as a business and learn to accept losses.

Trading in the stock market can be as effective and profitable as you can make it. There's no fixed mantra for success in trading because one size does not fit all. However, it is easy to find resources on the Internet and rectify your mistakes. You'll have to experiment with different stances and strategies to determine what works best for you. The bottom line is that you must not underestimate yourself, and you should always look for better settings, strategies and positions for your penny stock trading business.

References

Hayes, A. (2021, June 1). How does the stock market work? Retrieved from Investopedia.com website: https://www.investopedia.com/articles/investing/082614/how-stock-market-works.asp

More, R. (2021, March 15). Stock Analysis: An Introduction. Retrieved from Nerdwallet.com website: https://www.nerdwallet.com/article/investing/stock-analysis-for-beginners

AAPL Stock Price. (n.d.). Retrieved from Marketwatch.com website: https://www.marketwatch.com/investing/stock/aapl

Apple - 41-year stock price history. (n.d.). Retrieved from Macrotrends.net website: https://www.macrotrends.net/stocks/charts/AAPL/apple-stock-price-history

CANN Stock Price. (n.d.). Retrieved from Marketwatch.com website: https://www.marketwatch.com/investing/stock/cann

EVC Stock Price. (n.d.). Retrieved from Marketwatch.com website: https://www.marketwatch.com/investing/stock/evc

Graham, B. (1972). The Intelligent Investor (4th ed.). HarperCollins.

Leeds, P. (n.d.-a). Specific factors are driving the prices of penny stocks. Retrieved from Thebalance.com website: https://www.thebalance.com/factors-driving-penny-stock-prices-4072794

Leeds, P. (n.d.-b). Top Pot and Marijuana-Related Penny Stocks. Retrieved from Thebalance.com website: https://www.thebalance.com/top-marijuana-penny-stocks-4110440

Liquidity meaning (what is liquidity?): Types & importance of liquidity – Franklin Templeton india®. (n.d.). Retrieved from Franklintempletonindia.com website: https://www.franklintempletonindia.com/investor/investor-education/video/term-busters-liquidity-io040g31

Matthew Frankel, C. F. P. (n.d.). Over-the-counter (OTC) stock market definition. Retrieved from Fool.com website: https://www.fool.com/investing/stock-market/exchange/otc-markets/

MNST Stock Price. (n.d.). Retrieved from Marketwatch.com website: https://www.marketwatch.com/investing/stock/mnst

Monster Beverage net worth 2006-2021. (n.d.). Retrieved from Macrotrends.net website: https://www.macrotrends.net/stocks/charts/MNST/monster-beverage/net-worth

Moskowitz, D. (2021, May 19). The risks and rewards of penny stocks. Retrieved from Investopedia.com website: https://www.investopedia.com/updates/penny-stocks-risks-rewards/

Stanger, M. (2012, October 5). What are the odds of your Startup succeeding? [INFOGRAPHIC]. Business Insider. Retrieved from https://www.businessinsider.com/the-odds-of-startup-success-2012-10

The ultimate guide to penny stocks: What they are and how they work. (2020, October 12). Retrieved from Daglar-cizmeci.com website: https://daglar-cizmeci.com/penny-stocks/

Williams, S. (2019a, October 17). Canada legalizes marijuana derivatives today: 6 things you need to know. Retrieved from The Motley Fool website: https://www.fool.com/investing/2019/10/17/canada-legalizes-marijuana-derivatives-today-6-thi.aspx

Williams, S. (2019b, December 22). 10 reasons marijuana stocks were pummeled in 2019. Retrieved from The Motley Fool website: https://www.fool.com/investing/2019/12/22/10-reasons-marijuana-stocks-were-pummeled-in-2019.aspx

(N.d.). Retrieved from Usnews.com website: https://money.usnews.com/investing/investing-101/articles/what-to-know-about-trading-penny-stocks

Abhishek, K. (2021, March 17). How to choose a stockbroker? 10 ultimate tips for beginners! Retrieved from Tradebrains.in website: https://tradebrains.in/how-to-choose-a-stockbroker/

Stockbroker. (2020, October 31). Retrieved from Corporatefinanceinstitute.com website: https://corporatefinanceinstitute.com/resources/knowledge/trading-investing/stockbroker/

Today, S. Z. (2014, April 19). How to choose the right broker for investment guidance. Retrieved from Business Today website: https://www.businesstoday.in/moneytoday/investment/tips-to-choose-right-broker-brokerage-house-for-investment/story/204742.html.

Why do you need a stock broker for trading in Indian stock market ::Sharetipsinfo.com. (n.d.). Retrieved from Sharetipsinfo.com website: https://www.sharetipsinfo.com/why-we-need-stock-broker.html

Cameron, R. (2016, December 22). Penny stocks trading guide for beginners [2021]. Retrieved from Warriortrading.com website: https://www.warriortrading.com/penny-stocks/

Leeds, P. (n.d.). Beginner's guide to trading penny stocks. Retrieved from Thebalance.com website: https://www.thebalance.com/penny-stocks-trading-guide-for-beginners-4123635

12 stock chart patterns you need to learn, & examples. (2019, November 7). Retrieved from Stockstotrade.com website: https://stockstotrade.com/chart-patterns/

Harmon, J. (2019, July 2). What's a good catalyst for trading penny stocks? Retrieved from Stocktraderjack.com website: https://stocktraderjack.com/whats-a-good-catalyst-for-trading-penny-stocks/

Penny Stocks: What Factors Affects these Stocks? (2019, March 17). Retrieved from Knowonlineadvertising.com website: https://www.knowonlineadvertising.com/beyond-digital/penny-stocks-what-factors-affects-these-stocks/

Mishra, D. (2020, July 13). How to pick winning penny stocks? Step by step guide. Retrieved from Groww.in website: https://groww.in/blog/how-to-pick-winning-penny-stocks/

Murphy, C. (2021, April 26). How to pick winning penny stocks. Retrieved from Investopedia.com website: https://www.investopedia.com/articles/investing/092214/how-pick-winning-penny-stocks.asp

fb.com/investorslive. (2021, April 28). Penny stock trading guide - 30 rules for OTC traders. Retrieved from Investorsunderground.com website: https://www.investorsunderground.com/penny-stock-trading-guide/

Murphy, C. (2021, April 26). How to pick winning penny stocks. Retrieved from Investopedia.com website: https://www.investopedia.com/articles/investing/092214/how-pick-winning-penny-stocks.asp

Sincere, M. (2012, February 3). 10 ways to trade penny stocks. Retrieved from MarketWatch website: https://www.marketwatch.com/amp/story/10-ways-to-trade-penny-stocks-2012-02-03

TradingStrategyGuides. (2019, July 3). Penny stocks for beginners (trading with just $100). Retrieved from Trading Strategy Guides website: https://tradingstrategyguides.com/penny-stocks/

Little, K. (n.d.). The Top Tools of Fundamental Analysis. Retrieved from Thebalance.com website: https://www.thebalance.com/tools-of-fundamental-analysis-3140772

Segal, T. (2021, June 10). Fundamental Analysis. Retrieved from Investopedia.com website: https://www.investopedia.com/terms/f/fundamentalanalysis.asp

Seth, S. (2021, April 29). Technical analysis strategies for beginners. Retrieved from Investopedia.com website: https://www.investopedia.com/articles/active-trading/102914/technical-analysis-strategies-beginners.asp

Technical analysis - beginner's guide to technical charts. (2018, February 6). Retrieved from Corporatefinanceinstitute.com website: https://corporatefinanceinstitute.com/resources/knowledge/trading-investing/technical-analysis/

Trading risk management: Rules & techniques for traders. (2020, October 5). Retrieved from Stockstotrade.com website: https://stockstotrade.com/trading-risk-management/

Moskowitz, D. (2021, May 19). The risks and rewards of penny stocks. Retrieved from Investopedia.com website: https://www.investopedia.com/updates/penny-stocks-risks-rewards/

Caster, A. (2021, June 5). Guide to risk management in OTC markets and playing penny stocks - all peers. Retrieved from Allpeers.com website: https://www.allpeers.com/guide-to-risk-management-in-otc-markets-and-playing-penny-stocks/

Sykes, T. (2018, April 30). 8 common penny stock trading mistakes. Retrieved from Wallstreetdaily.com website: https://www.wallstreetdaily.com/2018/04/30/8-common-penny-stock-trading-mistakes/

13 trading mistakes to avoid at all costs. (2014, March 16). Retrieved from Timothysykes.com website: https://www.timothysykes.com/blog/common-trading-mistakes/

3 common mistakes investors make with penny stocks. (2021, April 30). Retrieved from Fool.co.uk website: https://www.fool.co.uk/investing/2021/04/30/3-common-mistakes-investors-make-with-penny-stocks

www.ingramcontent.com/pod-product-compliance
Ingram Content Group UK Ltd.
Pitfield, Milton Keynes, MK11 3LW, UK
UKHW021311180426
11947UKWH00015B/1150